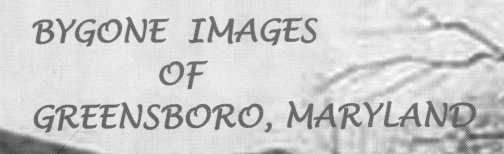

BYGONE IMAGES
OF
GREENSBORO, MARYLAND

Greensboro Historical Society;
Chapter of the Caroline County Historical Society, Inc.

Order this book online at www.trafford.com
or email orders@trafford.com

Most Trafford titles are also available at major online book retailers.

Printed in the United States of America.

ISBN: 978-1-4269-9631-3 (sc)
ISBN: 978-1-4269-9632-0 (e)

Trafford rev. 11/02/2011

www.trafford.com

North America & international
toll-free: 1 888 232 4444 (USA & Canada)
phone: 250 383 6864 ♦ fax: 812 355 4082

Bygone Images

Of

Greensboro

Greensboro Historical Society
Chapter of the Caroline County Historical Society, Inc.

ACKNOWLEDGEMENTS

The Greensboro Chapter of the Caroline County Historical Society recognizes the following members with special thanks for the contribution of their time, ideas, research, memories and loan of artifacts and pictures which have served to make this book possible. This publication is dedicated to the past, present, and future generations of the Town of Greensboro.

The Book Committee:

Ms. Betty J. Ballas   Mr. William F. Gray

Mr. Hugh R. Butler   Mr. Gale P. Nashold

Ms. Jo Ann Dean   Ms. S. Denise Quinn

Ms. Mary Lou Riddleberger

Cover: Home of Peter Rich, early founder. Ca 1755

INTRODUCTION

The area that now encompasses Greater Greensboro has a history of habitation that dates to pre-historic times. The area was inhabited by Indians of the Nanticoke tribes long before the arrival of settlers from the "Old World" countries. European colonists, fur trade wars and the infamous "Walking Purchase" of 1737 displaced many of these local Indians. In 1732, the Maryland Assembly passed an act to establish a town at the bridge on the Great Bend of the Choptank River. Peter Rich then patented thirty-one acres of land at Choptank Bridge for the purpose of establishing a community called Bridge Town. Peter Rich and his grandson, Peter Harrington, became the founders of Bridge Town, which became known as Greensborough in 1791.

This book comes to you from the Greensboro Historical Society and is intended to encourage others to learn more about the rich and varied history of our town and the surrounding area. We view this publication as the second phase of a three phase process which is intended to culminate in the publication of a more comprehensive history of Greensboro and its environs. We will begin the narrative with the Choptank Indians and end in twenty-first century Greensboro. The first phase of this process yielded the 2007 publication of a walking tour in recognition of the 275th anniversary of the founding of our town. These publications may still be available at the museum in Greensboro located at 114 W. Sunset Avenue.

The second phase of the process is this first volume which includes historic photos and captions taking you through the late nineteenth and mid-twentieth centuries. In the interest of finally getting this book to the publisher, some other items received through the generosity of many local folks will not be included here but will be included in the next edition of this volume.

The third phase will be the publication of a comprehensive history of the Greensboro area from pre Columbian times to the present day.

We hope you enjoy reading this volume as much as we have enjoyed preparing it. We welcome the participation of anyone who may have an interest in contributing to the preparation and publication of our next issue.

Greensboro Chapter of the Caroline County Historical Society
Gale P. Nashold, President

CONTENTS

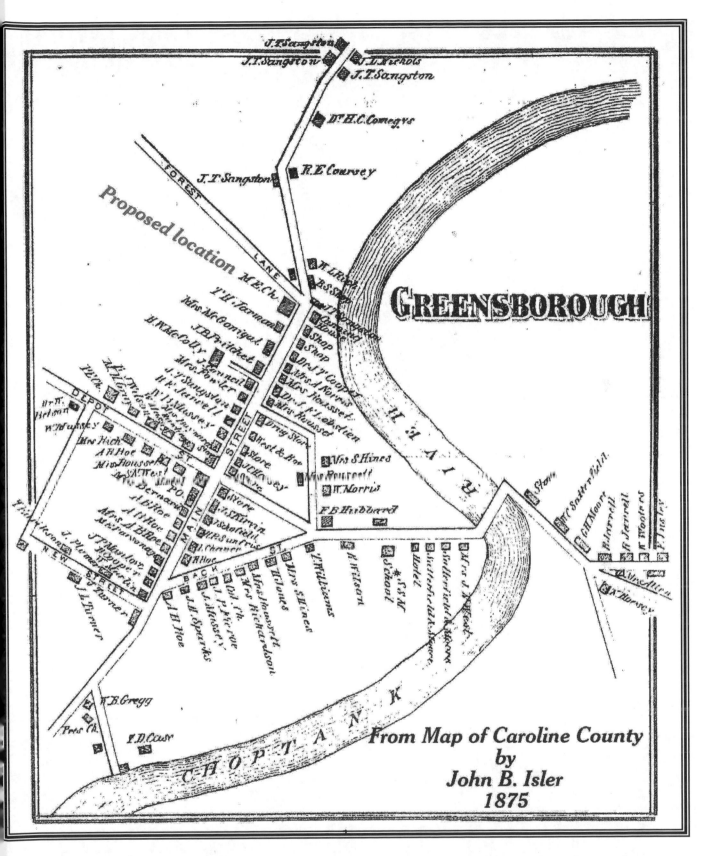

This inset from the 1875 Map of Greensborough, created by John B. Isler, shows the landowners of Greensborough during the later years of the 19th century. It also shows the present-day location of the Greensboro Historical Society's Visitors' Center and mini-museum for the Town of Greensboro. (Map ~ Greensboro Museum)

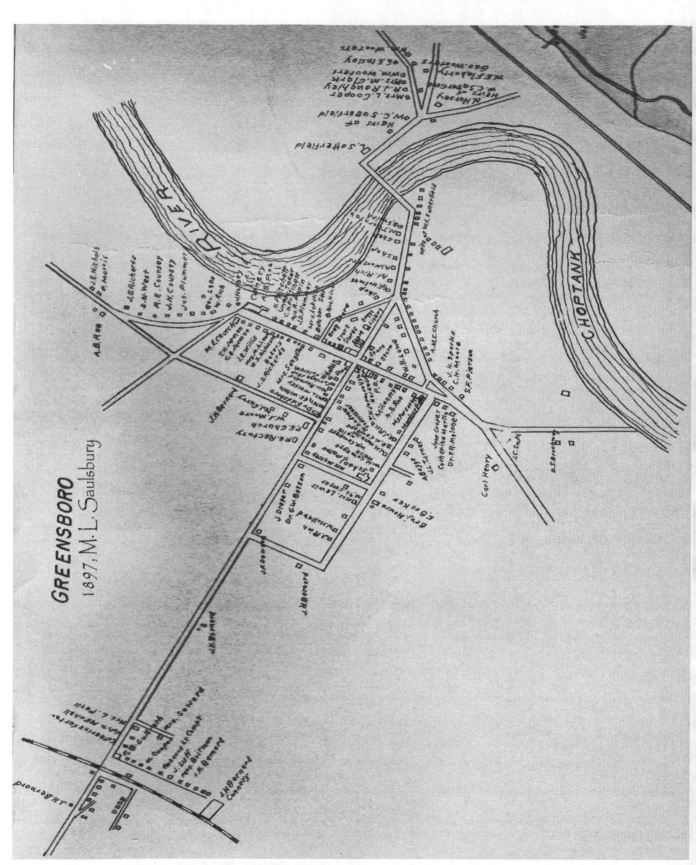

This Greensboro inset from the 1897 Map of Caroline County was created by M. L. Sauls-bury, Civil Engineer. Shown are the property owners of Greensboro 22 years after the 1875 Map from the preceding page. (Map ~ Greensboro Museum)

A RHYME OF BYGONE YEARS

Listen, good people, and you shall hear
The story of many a bygone year,
Reaching back to the days of yore
When Indians wandered on Eastern Shore.
Even to sixteen-hundred eight (1608)
When Smith explored the Eastern state.

Once more, five years ere Baltimore came
Claibourne exploring found again
Metapeake, Nanticoke, and Choptank,
Lurking in forests deep and dank.

Sixteen-hundred sixty-nine (1669)
This is the year in which I find
Governor Calvert—Charles by name
Granted the Indians certain claim
To lands. These they could call their own
A "Reservation"." The Indians home.
Six beaver skins they yearly sent
To the Lord Proprietor for rent.

For sixteen-hundred eighty-three (1683)
.An interesting chapter see.
To the home of William Troth one day
A drunken Indian chanced to stray,
He, both with tomahawk and gun,
Tried for Troth's life—Then away he run.

The trial came, Court judgment sent
The Indian far. 'Twas, "Banishment".
On the Court records e'en todoay is
The noted trial of Poh Poh Caquis.

Years passed. In seventeen-hundred four (1704)
The rising power of the white man bore
The Red man backward through forest glade,
'Twas then the Nanticoke Treaty was made.
So civilization rose like the tide
And the Indians were scattered far and wide.

As time rolled on the traffic grew,
And so, in seventeen thirty-two (1732)
The government granted the people right
To plot a town on Greensboro's site,
A bridge across the river was thrown,
Accordingly it was called Bridgetown.

Twenty acres in Dorchester lay
Per acre twenty-four shillings they pay,
Twenty more by Queen Anne were given
Shillings per acre, twenty-seven,
And the purchasers paid for years,--oh many
The Lord Proprietor a tax of one penny.
Such is the story I tell to you
Of Greensboro.—Seventeen thirty-two. (1732)

In fifty-six Arcadians came (1756)
The Huguenot French well known to fame,
Who knows but some fair Evangeline
At Bridgetown crossing was oftimes seen.

Then just before the birth of our Nation
Caroline County was given foundation,
Made from Queen Anne and Dorchester—
Talbot also formed part of her.
Caroline Calvert, the name was for,
Wife of Lord Eden, the Governor
Who served the King on Eastern Shore
The year of our Lord, seventeen-seventy-four. (1774)

Soon was the Revolution here
With its midnight ride of Paul Revere.
Soliders were gathering by the score,
And Caroline added one company more.

What found we then in a soliders pack?
What carried he in his haversack?
One half pound powder; a bag of ball;
Two pounds of lead, Nor was this all,
A cartridge box filled with cartouch;
A powder horn. What more could you wish
Except his flintlock with trigger set,
And barrel pointed by bayonet
Some of the bravest no doubt were found,
Carrying guns made from old Bridgetown
Then, they made the English run,
Just as yesterday they made the Hun.

Seventeen hundred ninety-one (1791)
War was over. Peace had come.
The State Assembly authorized
That Bridgetown be reorganized.
The old town stood as heretofore
But added one hundred acres more
Purchased from lands on the Western bank
Where the bridge led over the old Choptank.
There on an Indian summer day
Old Bridgetown was laid away.
The new town born was called I trow
By its present name of Greensboro.
Both records and folk-lore prove I ween
That the town was named for one Valentine Green.
Then at a date that has not appeared
A Presbyterian Church was reared.

You know the rest,--How Greensboro through
The following century steadily grew,
How in eighteen-eight (1808) a new bridge was thrown
Over the Choptank. The old was down,
How eighteen-sixteen (1816) Public School
And free education became the rule,
Then at a date that has not appeared
A Presbyterian Church was reared.

Later Episcopal and M. E.
Were added to Greensboro's family tree.
In eighteen-twenty-five (1825) you get
Your medicine from Dr. Rousset.
In 1880 a newspaper. Guess?
Why of course the Greensboro Free Press.
Railroad, factories, canneries came.
Now Greensboro is known to fame.

Here's a toast. May her fame spread far and wide
Then, higher rise,.like a Choptank tide.
And though in distant lands we roam
May we eér be proud to call Greensboro—Home.

Recited by BESSIE EDWARDS

From the "History of Caroline County Maryland"
Teachers and Children of the County
1920

HOUSES

&

STREETS

Home of Peter Rich. This home was located on the east side of the Choptank River and was attached to a mercantile business of Peter Rich, a town founding father . Built circa 1755 on Lot #21 which was one of the original forty lots that were laid out in 1732 "in and immediately across from the Great Bend of Choptank River."
(photo~ Hugh R. Butler collection)

Home of Peter Harrington. This circa 1920 photograph shows one of the historic buildings that has survived from Greensboro's early years. Peter Harrington and his grandfather Peter Rich were the founders of what would later be known as the town of Greensboro. The original home is primarily of brick construction and was built circa August of 1786. It may still be seen today at 200 Church Street.

During the Revolutionary War, Peter Harrington served in 1777 as an Ensign in the militia, Capt. Thomas Hughlett's Company, 28th Battalion and served in 1778 as a Second Lieutenant. He was appointed Constable of Bridgetown Hundred (which included present day Greensboro) in 1778. In 1782 he was credited with rendering patriotic service by providing wheat for the use of the military. (Revolutionary Patriots of Caroline County Maryland 1775-1783 by Henry C. Peden, Jr.)
(photo~ Hugh R. Butler collection)

Nehemiah's Tavern.: Nehemiah Townsend was an innkeeper in the building shown above on Lot #15 of the original plat of the town. In 1793, Townsend was one of the commissioners that were appointed to oversee the construction of the replacement bridge across the Choptank in Greensboro. This was the second oldest house in Caroline County .
(photo & story ~ page 8—part 2, Section 3 of the Baltimore Sun, January 9, 1927; Article entitled "Caroline County A Garden Spot Of State")

Ailanthus Gateway. This house on S. Main Street was built before 1800, when the owner brought his bride to town and planted two slender trees, one on either side of the gateway. Over the years, the trees grew until their trunks and branches formed an archway, beneath which swung a gate. The trees have long since disappeared, and only a very few images remain to remind us of one the many pieces of history attached to this town. The building with the shutters was the first Bank of Greensboro. To the right of the trees is Reed's Big Store. (photo~ Hugh R. Butler collection)

Old Parsonage. This home at 308 N. Main Street was built circa 1832 to serve as the Methodist parsonage in Greensboro. This building is the only structure in Greensboro that is listed on the National Registry of Historical Homes. (photo~ Brud & Elsie Embert collection)

Main Street of Greensboro: Northeast corner of Main Street and Sunset Avenue circa 1900. The building on the left is one of the hotels in town at the start of the 20th century. On the right end of the building is a general store. Today this is the location of gas pumps and a parking lot for a convenience store. (photo~ Hugh R. Butler collection)

Main Street View of Ailanthus Gateway. Looking north toward Four Corners, this circa 1900 view of Main Street shows the two **ailanthus** trees in the left center of the photograph. The old Post Office is at far left; at the far right is the present day Greensborough Trading Company. (photo~ Hugh R. Butler collection)

Home of Edwards Family. This photograph was taken looking east on W. Sunset Avenue and School Street. It was the home of Norman and Katie Edwards. (photo~ Hugh R. Butler collection)

Home Owned by Andrew B. Roe. This home was built at 110 S. Main Street in 1888 for Andrew B. Roe, a local architect, canner and State Senator. (photo~ Hugh R. Butler collection)

Home of Frederick P. Roe. This home built in 1903 was located at 118 S. Main Street. It was the new home of local canner Frederick P. Roe . The canning business was operated by F. P. Roe from 1900 to 1941. The Quaker Meeting House which was used for monthly meetings of the Third Haven can be seen in the left background. (photo~ William F. Gray)

Home of Dr. Frederick P. Malone, M.D. This circa 1875 structure at 204 S. Main Street was the home of Dr. Frederick P. Malone, a local physician, President of the Medical Society of Caroline County, vestryman of Holy Trinity P.E. Church and served as a Greensboro Town Commissioner. (photo~ Hugh R. Butler collection)

Home of Dr. William W. Goldsborough. This early 19th century building became the home of Dr. William W. (grandson of Dr. G.W. Goldsborough) and subsequently his brother, Judge W. Laird Goldsborough. 116 W. Sunset Ave. (Photo~ Eric Goldsborough collection)

Home of Captain Cornelius Comegys. This home was located at N. Main and Church Streets. Captain Comegys was a prominent businessman involved in mercantile, shipping, lumber, tanning, and shoe manufacturing. His son, Dr. Henry C. Comegys studied under Dr. G.W. Golsborough prior to attending University of Maryland and subsequently returned to Greensboro to open his own medical practice. During the Civil War, he served as an assistant surgeon at Hamon General Hospital at Point Lookout. (photo~ Hugh R. Butler collection)

The Massey / Brumbaugh / Boulais House. This 109 N. Main Street home is the only surviving townhouse in Greensboro. The two-story wing to the north side (right) is the original 1790 structure. The young girl on the right is Mae Pippin. (photo~ Hugh R. Butler collection)

Home of Burt Hobbs. This home is located at the intersection of Hobbs Street & West Sunset Avenues. Burt Hobbs was involved in many business enterprises (general store, coal business, feed business, etc.) in the town of Greensboro. (photo~ Richard Porter collection)

Home of Clinton B. Jarman, located at 204 N. Main Street. C. B. Jarman inherited his father's hardware business and became a wealthy and influential businessman of 19-century Greensboro. He also built the Riverside Hotel across the street by renovating and expanding the Old A. B. Roe Cannery. Other family members shown in this photograph are Clinton's father (Thomas) and Clinton's son (Clinton B. Jarman, Jr.). (photo~ Hugh R. Butler collection)

*Home of the Clinton B. Jarman family. The Tom Jarman family is seen in front of their residence that is l*ocated on N. Main Street, built in 1891. (photo~ Hugh R. Butler collection)

Home of R.B. Culbreth. This home, located at 104 W. Sunset Avenue, served as a board-inghouse for teachers at the local school during the late 19th and early 20th centuries. (photo~ Hugh R. Butler collection)

Home of Benjamin House / Harry Bastian and the Photo Studio. The dwelling on the left was built in the early 1890's as the home of Benjamin House and his family. Benjamin House was a veteran of the Union Navy during the American Civil War (known by some as "The war of Northern Aggression").

The small building on the right was used as a photographer's studio and was the home of three different photographers over many years. Benjamin House was the first to use it as a photographer's studio, followed by Davis and then by Harry Bastian, who was the son-in-law of Benjamin House.

Over the years many other uses were found for the small house including a place for a men's club to meet, a practice room for the Greensboro Town Band and a small-scale apartment for newly weds. The home on the left is still located at the intersection of Maple Avenue & School Street.

The small building on the right was donated to the Greensboro Historical Society by Mr. and Mrs. William Strotman. The historical society has relocated this building to the old Methodist Cemetery lot at the intersection of North Main Street and Cedar Lane. The building will be restored and used as a visitors center and a mini museum which will contain revolving exhibits of local history. (photo~ Hugh R. Butler collection)

RIVERDEEN: This house was initially built as the summer home of Addison A. Christian who was General Manager of Gimbel's Department Store in Philadelphia. It is located on the east side of the Choptank River at the intersection of Route 313 and 314. After Mr. Christian's death, Riverdeen, for many years, became the home of the G. Harrison and Annie Hooper Nashold family. The Nasholds sold the home to a Mrs. Steward who turned it into a maternity hospital in which many of Greensboro's baby boomers were born. The home is now occupied and is being renovated by the current owners, Mr. & Mrs. John Irby. (photo~ Gale P. Nashold collection)

Home of John S. Mitchell. This home, built in 1889, is located behind *Riverdeen.* Mrs. J. S. (Ida) Mitchell was the oldest daughter of William C. Satterfield who owned one of the warehouses near the Choptank River bridge. Mr. Satterfield was also in the mercantile and shipbuilding business with George H. Moore. (photo~ Hugh R. Butler collection)

Home of Captain Daniel S. Brockway. Captain Brockway was owner and operator of a line of steamers that transported people and farm produce to market in Baltimore on a weekly basis. Captain Brockway went on to build a flour mill near his Choptank River steamboat wharf. The Brockway family and servants are pictured under the tree on the right. The home, which is located at 114 Riverview Lane, became the home of the Linwood Riddleberger family who also became the owners of Brockway's Mill. (photo~ Hugh R. Butler collection)

Home of M.M. Andrews. M. M. Andrews was the local undertaker and cabinetmaker. Mr. and Mrs. Andrews are seen on the porch. This home is located at 111 W. Sunset Avenue. (photo~ Hugh R. Butler collection)

Home of Dr. George W. Betson. Practicing medicine around 1865, Dr. Betson was active in various town organizations including the Howard and Corsica Masonic Lodge. This photograph shows the rear of Dr. Betson's house on W. Sunset and Academy Streets. The summer kitchen has been relocated on the same property. (photo~ Hugh R. Butler collection)

Family Home?? This home was located on the corner of what is currently known as East Sunset Avenue and Stonesifer Drive. The historical society is attempting to determine the identity of the family shown in this photograph. The house is no longer there. Assistance will be greatly appreciated. (photo~ William F. Gray)

Home of the Norman Scott Family. The family is in front of their home that is located at west end of Maple Avenue. (photo~ Hugh R. Butler collection)

Home of the W. H. Weer Family. This is the home of W.H. Weer, located on Union Road. It was originally the Jerome Davis home, one of the largest strawberry farms on Maryland's Eastern Shore. (photo~Weer collection)

Thornton's Blacksmith Shop. By the 1920's, small blacksmith shops, such as the one on the far right, were still run by Greensboro residents such as Wilson Thornton and his wife. Their home was located on the river side of E. Sunset Avenue at what is now a small parking lot East of the small pavilion. (photo~ Hugh R. Butler collection)

Intersection of Main Street and Sunset Avenue (formerly Railroad Avenue) in Greensboro. Known as "the four corners". The low sign on the corner announces the feature playing at the "New Theatre" down the street. (photo~ Fay Hubbard)

Church and homes on W. Sunset Avenue: From left to right, the Methodist Parsonage, St. Paul's United Methodist Church, #210 is the Nathaniel Horsey home, and #208 is the Clayton Horsey / John Brown / Gale Nashold home. (ca. 1907). (photo~ Hugh R. Butler collection)

Home of Frank Usilton Family. This home was located at 102 S. Academy Street near Maple Avenue, and was demolished in 2010, and replaced with a new home. (photo~ Hugh R. Butler collection)

South Main Street looking North toward the "Four Corners". Third from left is the old Greensboro Post Office. On the right is John Brown's hardware store, currently (2011) the town hall. (photo~ Hugh R. Butler collection)

*North Main Street from the "Four Corners" (*intersection of Main St. and Sunset Ave.). Hotel at left was on the present site of the BB&T Bank. (formerly the "Caroline County Bank"). (photo~ Hugh R. Butler collection)

N. Main Street from the "four corners". This is looking north. On the left is the Massey-Brumbaugh - Boulais House and directly across the street on the right is the Lobstein Building (presently Gray's Appliances). Circa 1912. (photo~ Hugh R. Butler collection)

From S. Main Street.; looking north from what is now the Greensborough Pharmacy, ca 1930. The Caroline County Bank and the American Store can be seen on the left past the "four corners" intersection. (photo~ Hugh R. Butler collection)

North Main Street, looking North. (circa 1900). Pippin boarding house can be seen at the end of the street. (photo~ Hugh R. Butler collection)

North Main Street. Looking north from the Four Corners. Early hotel is on the left.
(photo~ Hugh R. Butler collection)

W. Sunset Ave. (formerly Railroad Avenue), looking west from the Four Corners. Caroline County Bank on the right; Neamiah Townsend's tavern on the left. (photo~ Hugh R. Butler)

W. Sunset Avenue at School Street looking east. The home of Norman and Katie Edwards is seen on the near left. (photo~ Hugh R. Butler collection).

Greensboro Residents

William C. Satterfield. (1822-1896)
Pictured at left is William Satterfield, one of Greensboro's leading citizens who owned a cannery, twenty-eight homes, a sawmill, and several thousand acres of timberland, he was principal partner in the shipbuilding firm and *the mercantile business* of Satterfield & Moore *in East Greensboro,*. (photo~ Hugh R. Butler collection)

George H. Moore. (1826-1898) This artist's sketch of George H. Moore portrays one of Greensboro's prominent citizens in the 19th century. During the shipbuilding phase of the town's history, Moore was a partner in *Satterfield & Moore Shipbuilders and the mercantile business in East Greensboro.* He also served as Chief Judge of the Orphan's Court for Caroline County. (photo~ Gale P. Nashold collection)

Ephraim Doty (1839-1911). This circa 1890's photograph, taken by Greensboro photographer Henry Cohee, shows Ephraim Doty, an itinerant teacher of vocal music in Caroline County at the turn of the century. Mr. Doty's melodeon, which he used while teaching, is now in the Greensboro museum. (this photo and the melodeon compliments of Anna Mae Doty Carroll via her daughter Sharon Dean collection)

Lillie Doty (born 1875). This photograph of Ephraim Doty's daughter was taken by local photographer Benjamin House. Benjamin House's studio now belongs to the historical society and has been re-located to the old Methodist cemetery at the intersection of North Main St. and Cedar Lane. (photo~ Anna Mae Doty Carroll via Sharon Dean collection)

Joseph H. Bernard. (In 1871, Joseph
served as contractor for the complete
renovation of the old Methodist Church
in Greensboro. He opened a lumber-
yard and a cannery in 1873. With the
cooperation of Andrew B. Roe, he built
bridges for the Maryland and Delaware
Railroad. He acted as architect and
general contractor for many buildings
in Caroline County; e.g., the new
Methodist Church in Greensboro, the
county court house and the old Peoples
Bank in Denton, the original buildings
at The Plains (St. Benedictine), and
more. (photo~ Hugh R. Butler collection)

Harry F. Butler: "H.F" was a former pastor and a long-time and well-known barber in the town of Greensboro. He was
very active with Greensboro baseball
teams. (photo~ Barbara B. Cain collection)

Dr. Griffin W. Goldsborough (1816-1902). Pictured right is the first of the Goldsborough family to reside at 116 W. Sunset Avenue. As one of the early physicians of Greensboro, he laid claim to a distinguished lineage, including Nicholas Goldsborough of Dorset, England who established the Goldsborough family of Maryland's Eastern Shore. G.W. studied medicine under Dr. Alward White of Greensboro and then continued his education at the University of Maryland, graduating in 1838. His first wife died in childbirth shortly after being rescued from a fire in the family manor house. G.W.'s hometown, Old Town, was renamed Goldsborough in his honor. A lifelong Episcopalian, he was instrumental in building the Episcopal Church in Greensboro. (photo~ Hugh R. Butler collection)

Dr. William Winder Goldsborough (1875-1943). William began his medical practice in Greensboro in 1902 with his grandfather, Dr. G.W. Goldsborough. An entrepreneur at heart, W. W. founded the *Caroline Sun* newspaper in Ridgely, publishing the first edition on March 15, 1902. He was a member of the Oyster Commission and served as a state senator from 1906 to 1910. In the spring of 1903, W.W. was elected President of the Board of Town Commissioners. His other interests included Master Mason and vestryman of the Protestant Episcopal Church of Greensboro. (photo~ Harry Wyre collection)

56

John Harvey Coursey. Mr. Coursey was an early owner and operator of the National Brands Stores located on the S.E. corner of the intersection of Main Street and Sunset Avenue. (photo~ Mabel E. Rifle collection)

Mabel Williams Coursey. Wife of John Harvey Coursey. (photo~ Mabel E. Rifle collection)

Greensboro Businessmen. Pictured (left to right)—Emery Turpin, James Nichols, J.C. Smith; seated—Benjamin House, and Fred Quimby. (photo~ Hugh R. Butler collection)

Arthur W. Brumbaugh. Mr. Brumbaugh served in the Maryland House of Delegates from 1919 to 1921. He was appointed by Governor A.C. Ritchie to the Building Committee of the Greensboro Public School in 1920. He opened a general merchandise department store in Greensboro in partnership with the Rev. G.S. Rairigh in 1910. "A.W." operated his store (now "Gray's Gas) at the corner of North Main and Stonsifer drive until the 1960s. (photo~Roberta Leggett Estate)

Eating Ice Cream on a Choptank River Dock in Greensboro. Henry Cohee, local photographer, and his wife are pictured on the far left with other area residents enjoying ice cream. (photo~ Hugh R. Butler collection)

Parlor of the Benjamin House Home. This photograph shows the front room of the home of the Benjamin House family where they would gather to perform on the pump organ and violin. Pictured from left to right—Mary House, Benjamin House, and Josephine House. The house is at the intersection of Academy Street and Maple Avenue. (photo~ Hugh R. Butler collection)

Butcher Shop. A butcher shop stood at the intersection of Main Street & Stonesifer Drive, where the Greensboro Volunteer Firehouse is now located. To the left is the home of Dr. J. E. Lobstein, pharmacist. (photo~ Hugh R. Butler collection)

Judge W. Laird Goldsborough (1869-1958) and Katharine Egbert Goldsborough (1879-). The judge was a veteran of the Spanish-American War with service in Cuba and the Philippine Islands. He was the son of Washington Elwell Goldsborough and Martha Laird Goldsborough, and an older brother of the late Judge T. Alan Goldsborough and Dr. William Winder Goldsborough. He and his wife, "Miss Kitty," (daughter of General Henry Clay Egbert, who fell in action during the Philippine Insurrection) resided at 116 W. Sunset Avenue. A historical marker can be seen in front of their former home.
(photo~Harry Wyre collection)

He graduated with the degree LLB. from the University of Maryland Law School in May1890 and was admitted to the Maryland Bar in December of that year, and to the New York Bar in 1892, where he practiced law until the outbreak of the Spanish-American War.

After the troops were mustered out on June 30, 1901, he remained in the Philippines and served for 17 years in the Civil Government set up by Act of U. S. Congress as follows: Public Prosecutor under Provost Marshall General; Asst. Chief of Constabulary with rank of Colonel in charge of Visayas, Mindanao and Jolo District; City Attorney for Manila; Asst. Attorney General for Philippine Islands; Member of Commission to Compile Laws of Philippine Islands; Member of Code Committee to codify the laws of Philippines.

On April 1, 1904,he was appointed Associate Judge of Land Registration of the Philippines, in which Court he presided for 11 years until his return to U. S. in 1917 to practice law in Wilmington, Delaware, and later went to New York City as Counsel for the Columbia Graphaphone Company. In 1923, W. Laird Goldsborough was commissioned Lt. Colonel of Infantry, Maryland National Guard and entered the Army War College course in Washington, D. C.

After his retirement from the practice of law in Wilmington and New York City he served twice as President of the Town Commissioners of Greensboro.

Andrew B. Roe. (1830 – 1897) Andrew owned a cannery on N. Main Street in Greensboro in 1872. The cannery was renovated and converted to the Riverside Hotel by C.B. Jarman in 1912.
He served as a Maryland State Senator from 1882 to 1886.
Father of F. P. Roe.
(photo~ Hugh R. Butler collection)

Frederick P. Roe (1862-1926). Frederick owned the F. P. Roe Cannery from 1900 until it was destroyed by fire in 1941, the result of an accident with a blowtorch. He was very active in the town government during the early 20th century. It was under his leadership as President of the Town Council that the town's water, sewer, and electrical distribution systems were developed. Son of A. B. Roe (photo~ Hugh R. Butler collection)

63

Dr. Charles Hiram Stonesifer (1900-1978): Dr. Stonesifer served Greensboro and the surrounding areas for 50 years beginning in 1928 and ending with his death, while still practicing, in 1978. His commitment to his patients and medical practice became legend in Caroline County. (photo~ Caroline Dean collection)

Submitted by Larry C. Porter for the book prepared by the Greensboro Historical Society

I will begin this narrative by saying that Doctor Stonesifer brought me into the world on September 5, 1952. I arrived prematurely in a farmhouse outside of Greensboro and weighed in at around three pounds. "Doc" improvised an incubator by placing me in a shoe box lined with cotton and sitting me on the oven door. That was my introduction to a man who was loved, and revered by the people in Greensboro and the surrounding area in a way that I have never seen in my lifetime.

My relationship with the Doctor existed through the years with his treatment of colds, ear infections, stitches, and more frequently "physicals". The physical examinations were necessary for you to participate in school sports activities, and required the dreaded OFFICE VISIT. I prepared myself for the visit by getting a lot of sleep, getting plenty of reading material, and learning all of the town gossip I could so as not to be left out of conversations. You must realize that Doctor Stonesifer did not believe in appointments. He was prepared to stay in the office longer than anyone else so the waiting process began. You entered the office, took a seat in the chair farthest from his office door and waited until the patient in his office came out. When they exited, you got up and moved to the next chair, with that procedure followed until you reached the magic goal of his office door. This waiting period could last as long as 12 to 14 hours, with food and water deliveries made by Mother who would visit with other patients and catch up on the local news. No one was exempt from waiting, shooting victims were treated on the same schedule as someone with a cold. The fear in your gut was always there as well that the Doctor would slip out the back door to make a "home visit". If an extended period of time passed without anyone exiting the office, a designation was made by the oldest or most influential waiting room patient, that person would appoint someone to go outside to see if the Doctor's car was still there. Waiting for that person to come back in was like waiting for a firing squad, if he was gone, no one knew where or for how long. You just settled in and hoped you would be out of there before your next birthday. When the time finally came for you to enter the office, the examination went something like this.......(him) How's your Mother, (me) fine (him) how do you feel (me) fine (him) are you behaving yourself (me) no response. After some further examination, he pronounced you fit. When I asked him how much he was to be paid, he would look at me as if I was crazy and inform me that he would get up and down with Mother sometime in the future, you see money was not exactly a priority with the Doctor. His material needs were far outweighed by his dedication and service to the people of our town.

The Lobstein Family. Dr. John Edward Lobstein (back row, center) (1829-1892), was brought to Greensboro by Dr. Henry Rousett (1785-1871) and family in 1860. (Back row right is Dr. Malone). Dr. Lobstein devoted most of his medical attention to the pharmaceutical business and maintained a store for thirty-five years that was considered by some to be "one of the best pharmacies in Maryland." The pharmacy was in the building now occupied by Gray's Appliances and Gas. The house on the left is where the Greensboro Barbershop is now located. The building in the background is now the location of the Greensboro Volunteer Fire Company. (photo~ Hugh R. Butler collection)

George W. Nashold, 1858 (Wisconsin) - 1918 (Greensboro, MD)
G. Harrison Nashold, 1888 (Wisconsin) - 1945 (Greensboro, MD)
Mary S. Nashold, 1861 (Wisconsin) - 1939 (Greensboro, MD)

Nashold Family (photo, 1889). George W. Nashold (1858-1918), G. Harrison Nashold (1888-1945) and Mary Stone Nashold (1861-1939). The Nasholds arrived in Greensboro from Columbia County, Wisconsin via Ablemarle County, Virginia in June of 1915. George was a dairy farmer west of Greensboro off of what is now Harrington Road.. (photo~ Gale P. Nashold collection)

The Nashold Family at the Harrington Road dairy farm, ca 1915.. This photograph
shows (left to right) Doris, Walter McKinley, Mary Stone, Harrison, and George Nashold.
(photo~ Gale P. Nashold collection)

G. Harrison Nashold, Sr.: This circa 1930 photograph shows Harrison standing in front of Riverdeen, his home in East Greensboro. The leather leg guards were worn to protect the legs from snakebites. *(a habit developed from time spent in Virginia and Georgia before coming to Greensboro).*

Harrison Nashold, was an entrepreneur with many business interests on the East side of the Choptank River in Greensboro (AKA Brooklyn). His business enterprises were active from 1920 through the depression era of the 1930s and into the early 1940s providing employment for more than 50 local people during this critical period in our nation's history.

Business activities included: a trucking company for agribusiness and general hauling; a pickle factory; a service station which included gas, Good Year tires, groceries and a tavern; a dance hall; a feed store; partner in the Nashold-Vandergrift Coal Co.; and an automobile agency. (photo~ Gale P. Nashold collection)

Neighbors:. Many of the neighborhood children could be found playing in the yard at *Riverdeen.* This circa 1942 photograph shows (left to right)—Billy Minner, Teddy Nashold, Gale Nashold, "Muppy" Minner, unknown. (photo~ Gale P. Nashold collection)

Wyatt Family Members. Pictured (left to right)—Oscar Wyatt, Mary Moore Wyatt, and Leslie Wyatt. Oscar Wyatt owned and operated the feed store located on East Sunset Avenue. They are standing outside the home located 101 Church Street. This circa 1934 photograph shows the pipes on the outside of the house that were added to incorporate indoor plumbing. (photo~ Mary Lou Riddleberger collection)

The Linwood Riddleberger Family. This family portrait is an indication of the typical size of families in the 19th and 20th centuries. A successful businessman in the community, Linwood rented the Brockway Flour Mill and moved his family into the Brockway dwelling in 1916. He later purchased the mill and dwelling and operated the mill with two of his sons through the 1950s. His grandson, Tom Riddleberger, a contractor, served several terms as Greensboro's mayor from the 1990s through the start of the 21st century. (photo~ Mary Lou Riddleberger collection)

The Girlfriends. This circa 1948 photograph shows (far left, clockwise) Miriam Baynard, Margie Linhard, Emma Greeley, Clara Jarman and Phyllis Nashold (center) arriving for the day in Rehoboth Beach in their newly purchased vehicle —- the "Doodle Bug". (photo~ Miriam Baynard Binebrick collection.)

1929 Model "A" Ford. This circa 1948 photograph shows the vehicle purchased by the five girls on the preceding page. A crowd gathered on Main Street in Greensboro for the unveiling of the newly named "Doodle Bug." It was shared by the friends and made many trips to Rehoboth Beach in the late 1940's. (photo~ Mariam Baynard Binebrick collection)

The Dukes' Sisters. Carolyn and Elaine Dukes are seen playing in the snow in front of their family home known as "Garden of Roses". This home is an historic dwelling of the Boon family and is located West of the town of Greensboro. (photo~ Carolyn Dukes Spicher collection)

Calvin and Evelyn Butler. Calvin was a long-time barber in town and a Navy veteran. He is shown here with his sister Evelyn. They are children of H.F. Butler. He is a 1934 graduate of Greensboro High School. (photo ~ Barbara Butler Cain collection)

Anna Lee Butler and Peggy Wothers. This photograph shows Anna Lee Butler on far left while Peggy Quillen Wothers is pulling her children (David, Mike, and Jodie) in a wagon down Main Street. In the left background is the location of the Taylor House prior to renovation. (photo~ Barbara Butler Cain collection)

CHURCHES

&

SCHOOLS

The old Methodist Church: The first church to occupy this location was a wooden struc-ture built on property acquired from Peter Harrington by the Society of Methodists in 1789. Francis Asbury, the first Bishop of the Methodist Church in America, preached in the church on this site many times. The second church here was constructed of brick in 1832 and was the first brick church in the region. This church was attended by both White and Black residents. In 1872 the church was remodeled by Joseph H. Bernard to be as is shown in the photo above. After 1904, when the congregation moved to their new St. Paul's Methodist Church on Sunset Avenue this building was used by other church de-nominations. The Pilgrim Holiness were the last to use this facility until it was razed in the 1960's. (photo ~ Claudine McClyment collection)

Old Parsonage. This home at 308 N. Main Street was built circa 1832 to serve as the Methodist parsonage in Greensboro. The building is the only structure in Greensboro listed on the National Historical Registry of Homes. (photo ~ Brud & Elsie Embert collection)

Old Methodist Church. Located on N. Main Street @ Cedar Lane. The bell tower shown in this photograph was added in 1872 as part of a major renovation to the 1832 brick church. The Pippin House (sign on far left) was a boarding house on N. Main Street. (photo~Hugh Butler collection)

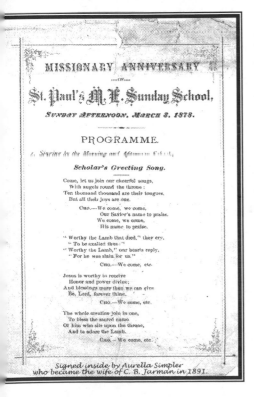

St. Paul's M.E. Sunday School Programme. Missionary Anniversary was celebrated in 1878 with a program featuring the morning and afternoon schools. The church is located at N. Main Street and Cedar Lane. (document ~Hugh R. Butler collection)

Rev. P. M. Shelton
1903 - 1909

Rev. Shelton built a new Church on the grounds where it
now is and named it Mt. Pleasant. Rev. Shelton was
also the person who first opened a school at
Ridgely, Maryland and taught there.

THE MINISTRY
1864-1998
Mount Pleasant Methodist Church

Rev. Harrison Rich & Rev. B. Green   1864~1865
No record of how long each pastor served.

Rev. David Eaves   ~   served 2 years. 1869

Rev. John A. Dennis   ~   A church builder. He built the first church in Greensboro for the exclusive use of the Negro residents and named it Dennis Temple, after himself and a local preacher, William Temple.

Rev. P.M. Shelton ~   served 6 years. He built the present church at a cost of $1400.00. It was dedicated as Mount Pleasant M. E. Church on May 28,1905. The congregation marched in the new church singing "We're Marching to Zion". The dedication service was preached by Rev. N. W. Moore, District Superintendent.

Rev. A. P. Jenkins ~   served 11 years, 1952-1963.
        Died as pastor, August 5, 1963.

Rev. John Ringgold   ~   served 2 years.

Rev. T. M. Murray ~   served 1 1/2 years.
        Died as pastor, April 27, 1970.

Rev. Lisa M. Graine   ~   2002 - ?

Dartanyon L. Hines   -   Present day (2011)

St. Paul's Methodist Episcopal Church. In 1904, growth of the Methodist congregation necessitated the building of a new church. Members obtained property two blocks west of downtown Greensboro and constructed a new, larger facility. The third Methodist church in Greensboro was built in 1904 under the direction of Rev. E.L. Hoffecker, D.D. and Joseph H. Bernard, local architect and leading layman. The house to the left of the church was erected as the parsonage in 1905. (photo ~Hugh R. Butler collection)

HARVEST HOME M.E.CHURCH,
GREENSBORO MD.

Sanctuary of St. Paul's Methodist Episcopal Church. This circa 1910 photograph of the annual Harvest Home celebration at St. Paul's Methodist Episcopal at W. Sunset Avenue is an illustration of the church Missions Committee's commitment to providing help for the needy. The organ in the far corner of the sanctuary was donated by contractor Joe Bernard. (photo ~Hugh R. Butler collection)

Church Sewing Circle. This circa 1910 photograph shows from left to right (front row) Mrs. E. Seward, Mrs. C. Clark, Mrs. F. Murphy, and Mrs. C. Butler; (middle row) Mrs. W. Wooters, Mrs. W. Sipple, Mrs. H. Jones, and Ms. Mae Cohee: (back row) Mrs. G. Wooters, Mrs. W. R. Bellow, Mrs. G. Nicholes, and Mrs. J. Jarvis. (photo ~ Hugh R. Butler collection)

St. Paul's Methodist Episcopal Church Junior Epworth League of 1919. Epworth Leagues were established by the Methodist Episcopal Church to ensure the spiritual welfare of young children. During the Civil War era, these leagues helped widows and orphans. (photo ~Hugh R. Butler collection)

Baptist Tabernacle. Prior to the building of the Baptist Church, (pictured on the follow-ing page), the congregation built and met at this tabernacle. The congregation was estab-lished in June 1920, and the first service was held in July of the same year. On July 5, a second service was held and the church was officially organized on November 1. Rev. Melvin G. Morris was pastor and there were twenty-four charter members. (photo~ Hugh R. Butler collection)

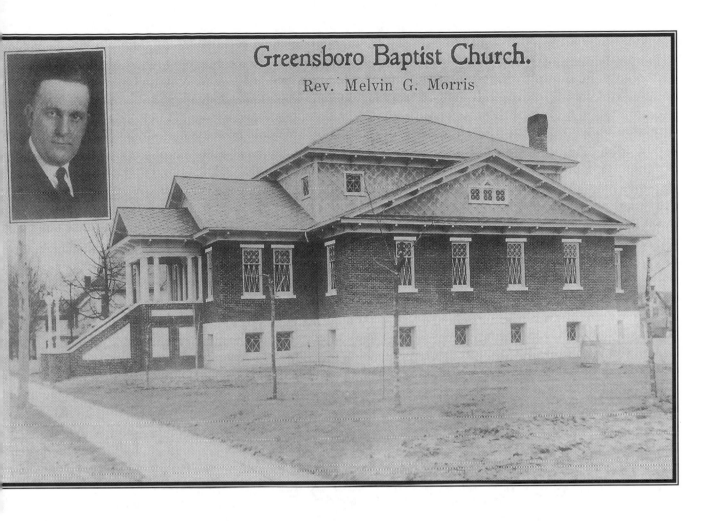

Greensboro Baptist Church.

Rev. Melvin G. Morris

Greensboro Baptist Church. Completed at a cost of $45,000, this structure was dedicated on February 10, 1924. The church suffered economically from 1935 to 1945 but was able to survive. On July 29, 1945, the congregation burned the mortgage. (photo~Hugh R. Butler collection)

Church of the Holy Trinity. This Episcopal church was established as the result of efforts of Angeline Goldsborough and Ella Betts. Mr. Ernst presented the idea of a new church to the convention in Easton, Maryland in 1870 and a new parish was formed. Building of the church was completed and dedicated on April 13, 1875. They formed a Sunday School. It was located at the corner of Church Street and W. Sunset Avenue, the present-day location of the U. S. Post Office in Greensboro. (photo~ Hugh R. Butler collection)

Sanctuary of Church of the Holy Trinity. This interior view of the sanctuary of Church of the Holy Trinity shows the detail of the altar area. (photo~ Hugh R. Butler collection)

Greensboro Cemetery. The Greensboro Cemetery Association was established in 1873. This picture of the Greensboro Cemetery is circa 1890. At that time, some remains from other burial sites were moved to this location. (photo~ Hugh R. Butler collection)

Moore's School and Pupils of 47 Years Ago

In 1856, Thomas Moore came from Sussex County, Delaware, where he bought a tract of land on the east side of the Choptank River near Greensboro, Md., to build a grist mill and saw mill. Mr. Moore saw the need for a school in that neighborhood succeeded, with the help of others, in getting a school built in 1857 or 58. This land was donated by Betsy Baynard. The first teacher in this one-room building was David Moore, a son of Mr. Thomas Moore. Therefore, the school became known as Moore's School. The building was later moved to a more central location, on land given by William Hutson. In 1912 this school could no longer accommodate the large crowd of children attending and a large room was built in front of the old one. The above picture was taken 47 years ago with John Weaver as teacher. Left to right, top row: Cordy Stokley, Amanda Boyd, Ernest Edwards, Eva Edwards, Robert Pinder, Florence Zweifle. Second row, John Sylvester, Elijah Hutson, Marley Pinder, Wiloughby Edwards, Cordy Stokley, Norman Edwards, Benny Rouse, Herbert Hutson, Jack Medford, Ada Hutson, Kellor Edwards, Bertha Camper, Fred Sylvester, Marshall Hutson, Nelson Bishop, Bertha Hutson, Mary Boyd. Third row: Harold Sylvester, Calvin Richard, Norman Walls, Harvey Wheeler, Louis Boyd, Henry Stokley, James Hutson, Eddie Stubbs, William Hubbard, Billy Baynard, Eva Bishop, Frank Pinder, Oscar Bishop, Mattie Hubbard, Elsie Bilbrough, Pearl Bilbrough, Ester Meredith, Libbie Hubbard, Sophie Baynard, Helen Bishop. The Pinder children had to walk three miles to school, this being the longest distance. Several were absent the day the picture was taken. About 1938 or 39 this building was purchased by Mr. W. T. Lockerman and is now being used for mixing and grinding rooms of The W. T. Lockerman Co. The picture was brought to The Record office by George Gottwals of Greensboro.

Moore's School was located North East of Greensboro near Draper's Mill Road.

Greensboro's Negro School. This elementary school was attended by the negro children prior to de-segregation in 1960. It is still standing today and serves as a residence on Mill Street. (photo ~Hugh R. Butler collection)

ACADEMY, GREENSBORO MD.

This Schoolhouse was on the NE corner of the intersection of Maple Avenue and Academy Street. The structure was built in 1872 with an addition in 1890s. The home of Col. William H. Comegys, Commander of troops from Caroline County during the Civil War, is seen in the right background. (photo~ Hugh R. Butler collection)

Back of Maple Avenue School. This view was of the back of the Maple Avenue School after the 1890's addition was finished. (photo~ Hugh R. Butler collection)

School Principal and Teachers. This circa 1913 photograph shows the Maple Avenue Academy principal Mr. Percy Simmons and teachers Miss Leacy Roe (second row left) and Miss Mary Butterworth (front row right) among other unidentified teaching staff members . (photo~ Hugh R. Butler collection)

1912 Girls' Tennis Team. Miss Butterworth (far left) coached the 1912 girls' high school tennis team at the Maple Avenue School. (photo~ Hugh R. Butler collection)

Greensboro School, grades 1 - 12.: This structure was built in 1920 as noted on the stone above the front door of the Greensboro School. This was an eleven year school until 1949 when a twelfth year was added ; the class of 1950 became the class of 1951. The first classes were held in 1922 with the last high school class graduating in 1959. From September 1959 until June 1974, the building served as Greensboro Elementary School. In 1986, the building opened as The Schoolhouse Apartments. (photo ~Hugh R. Butler collection)

1921 Girls' State Volleyball Champions. This photograph shows the Greensboro High School championship volleyball team of (front row L to R)—Mary Dill, Ruth Jackson, Grace Stuft, Bess Edwards; Back row—Katharine Kibler, Helen Bilbrough, Rebecca Lane, Anne Kibler. (photo ~Hugh R. Butler collection)

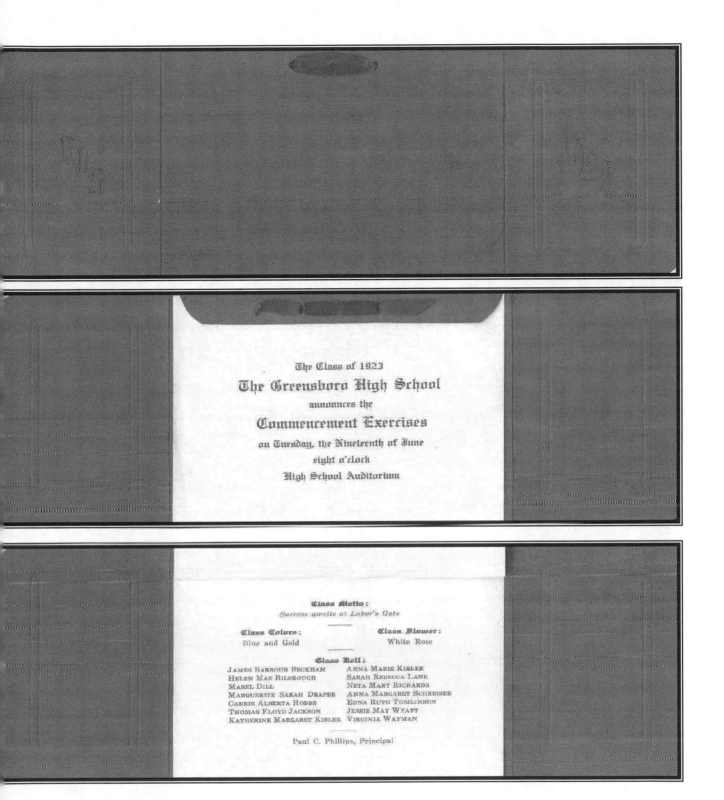

The Class of 1923

The Greensboro High School

announces the

Commencement Exercises

on Tuesday, the Nineteenth of June

eight o'clock

High School Auditorium

Class Motto:
Success awaits at Labor's Gate

Class Colors: **Class Flower:**
Blue and Gold   White Rose

Class Roll:

James Barbour Beckham   Anna Marie Kibler
Helen Mae Bilbrough   Sarah Rebecca Lane
Mabel Dill   Neta Mary Richards
Marguerite Sarah Draper   Anna Margaret Schreiber
Carrie Alberta Hobbs   Edna Ruth Tomlinson
Thomas Floyd Jackson   Jessie May Wyatt
Katherine Margaret Kibler   Virginia Wayman

Paul C. Phillips, Principal

Greensboro High School Class of 1923 Program. The first graduating class of Greensboro High School conducted their commencement exercises in the high school auditorium on June 19, 1923. Shown above are the class motto, class colors, class flower, and the fourteen students on the class roll. (Source ~ Greensboro High School reunion committee)

Stage Production at Mozart Hall.
Participants from the Greensboro
High School Class of 1924 perform
in a historic stage production at Mozart Hall. (L to R) in the picture to the
right: Strod Beckham, Katharine
Kibler, and Joe Bernard. The entire
cast of the play is shown on stage in
Mozart Hall in the picture above.
(photo ~Hugh R. Butler collection)

Greensboro School Library. This photograph shows high school students in the library of the Greensboro School located on School Street. (photo ~ Caroline County Board of Education collection)

Greensboro School Typing & Shorthand Class. Mr. G. B. Hastings, who later became principal in 1944, taught the typing class to high school students. (photo ~ Caroline County Board of Education collection)

May Day Celebration. Greensboro High School played host to the May Day celebration in 1953. In foreground (L to R)—Nancy Minner, Jean Griffin, unknown, Sheila Schreiber, Shelley Lewis. (photo~Mary Lou Riddleberger collection)

Royal Court of May Day. This circa 1954 photograph shows the Royal Court of the annual May Day celebration held at Greensboro School. Front row (L to R)—Mary Lou Wyatt, Sally Eash, Dickie Pursley, Dottie Stirn, and Margaret Eveland; second row—Sally Medford, Mary Carolyn Shockley, unknown, unknown, Barbara Ellwanger, Joe Germick, Henrietta Harris, Mary Kelly, Kenny Wothers, Ellen Cohee, Bill Gray, Janice Boulais, Carolyn Brown, Emily Ellwanger, Kathryn Schreiber, unknown. (photo~Mary Lou Wyatt Riddleberger collection)

Greensboro High School Glee Club. The 1952 Greensboro High School Glee Club per-
forms in a spring concert. INCLUDE NAMES OF THOSE LISTED ON DETAIL??
(photo~Jean Harris Basore collection)

H.M.S. Pinafore. This circa 1954 photograph shows the cast of *H.M.S. Pinafore*, a stage production that was performed by Greensboro High School. Part of the cast included Jane Harris and Doris Dill. (photo~Jean Harris Basore collection)

Greensboro High School Band led by Music Director Ms. Barbara Walters in the 1950's. The uniforms were worn in marching and concert band performances. (photos~JoAnn Riddleberger Dean collection)

High School Band and Music Director Ms. Barbara Walters (pictured at left) taught music in Greensboro High School in the 1950's. The uniforms were worn in marching and concert band performances. (photos~JoAnn Riddleberger Dean collection)

Greensboro High School 1932 Boy's Baseball Team. Front row (L to R)—Bradford Dickerson, Bill Cole, Ed Pearson, Bud Smith, Nelson Wyatt, Francis Meredith, Carlton Smith; Back row—Coach Duffy, Bill Terry, Lex Jarrell, Clarence Doty, Ed Hollingsworth, Howard Quillen, Fred Spence. (photo~ Hugh R. Butler collection)

Greensboro High School 1942 Boy's Basketball Team. Front row (L to R)—Willard Smith, George Stevenson, Robert Spence, Jack "Porky" Pritchett, Richard "Rusty" Rostien; Back row—Coach G.B. Hastings, Norman Draper "Big Dog" Usilton, C. L. "Shoog" Jarrell, Robert Kirwin, Merrell "Percy" Spence, Francis "Hatfield" Porter. (photo ~Hugh R. Butler collection)

Greensboro High School 1949 Boy's Soccer Champions. Front row (L to R)—Carl "Woody" Wibak, Bill Kriss, Bob Kriss, Nelson Henry, Frank "Jake" Usilton, Paul Wooleyhand, Mervin "Chunk" Usilton; Back row—Eddie Hobbs, Robert Shockley, Grayson Wheatley, Oscar Bishop, Richard "Muppy" Minner, Bob Stubbs, Eddie Wothers, Howard "T-bone" Tibbett, Kenny Wothers, Harry Turkington, Buck Hollingsworth, Bob Orrell, Tommy Bilbrough, Joe Germick, Billy Moyer, Coach Lacey. (photo~ Hugh R. Butler collection)

Greensboro High School 1953 Boy's Baseball County Champions. Front row (L to R)— Alan Bickling, Charles Dalrymple, Dickie Walls, Tinker Todd, George Nemith, Elmer Caine, James Porter, Mervin Cole; Back row—Lyle Dabson, Leroy Cahall, Allen Urry, Frank Usilton, Robert Dyer, Marvin Bolt, Paul Ward, Lloyd Nagai, David Ward, Wayne Butler, Coach Granville Diffie. (photo~ Hugh R. Butler collection)

Greensboro High School 1955 Girl's Basketball Team. Front row (L to R)—Marlene Hammer, Kay Schaub, Ruth Hayman, Faye Dill, Marie Wothers; Second row—Emily Ell-wanger, Phyllis Stubbs, Barbara Wyatt, Joyce Ann Nichols, Fay Butler, Ann Gray; Third row—Becky Longfellow, Virginia Bishop, Jackie Cartwright, Regina Hughes, UN-KNOWN, Columbia LePore; Fourth row—Janice Pippin, Coach Smith, Flo Sowada. (photo ~ Virginia Bishop Jones)

Greensboro High School 1955 Boys' Basketball Team. Front row (L to R)—Lowell Tho-
mas, Dinky Dabson, Jimmy Porter; Second row—Buck Thawley, Dave Ward, Elmer
Caine, Dicky Walls, Coach Diffie; Third row—Jimmy Richard, Joe Nemith, Lloyd Nagai,
Bobby Dyer. (photo~ Hugh R. Butler collection)

ROADWAYS

&

WATERWAYS

Brockway's Wharf. The wharf, at the end of present-day Riverview Lane, was home to many activities involved with river commerce. To the left is an oyster boat from Baltimore. The larger boat on the right is the *Walter P. Snow*. This circa 1880 scene depicts the loading and unloading of products, as well as boat maintenance. (photo ~Hugh R. Butler collection)

117

SS Greensborough. Frequent dredging of the Choptank River allowed local shipbuilders to construct local steamships like the *Greensborough*, as well as larger ocean-going vessels. The *Greensborough* served Chesapeake Bay routes until it was destroyed in a fire in 1907. (photo ~Hugh R. Butler collection)

SS Greensborough. This photograph shows the construction of the *SS Greensborough* in the 1880's with the workers at the Satterfield & Moore shipyard near the old Choptank River bridge. The steamer would travel to Baltimore on a weekly basis making stops at all landings between Greensborough and Cambridge. (photo~ Hugh R. Butler collection)

Remains of SS Greensborough.
The photograph on the above
shows the steamer while burning
in 1907. The remains of the hull
not destroyed by a fire in 1907 can
be seen as the *SS Greensborough*
is moved at Brockway's Wharf
(pictured on right) by the larger,
unnamed ship on its starboard
side. (photo ~Hugh R. Butler collection)

Waterway dredging. Maintaining the depth for river commerce and shipbuilding required frequent dredging. This circa 1878 photo was taken near the bridge at William C. Satterfield's warehouse. (photo~ Hugh R. Butler collection)

SS Edenton. River commerce on the Choptank River was not without its crises and accidents as evidenced by this circa 1910 image of the *SS Edenton* at Case's Wharf, with the wreck of the *SS Vesper* in the background. The *SS Vesper* was available for two weekly trips between Baltimore and wharves along the Eastern Shore of Maryland. Case's Wharf is at the end of present-day Mill Street in Greensboro. (photo ~Hugh R. Butler collection)

SS Plymouth. The circa 1910 photograph above is of the *SS Plymouth* that was owned by Elias and Minnie Kenton who are shown standing mid-ship. The *SS Plymouth* would soon meet with disaster by sinking into the Choptank River. (photo ~Hugh R. Butler collection)

Raising of the SS Plymouth. On the right, efforts to raise the steamship *SS Plymouth* appear to be futile.

Captain Benjamin House. One of Greensboro's prominent citizens, Capt. Benjamin House stands on the bow of his boat while on a solitary cruise down the Choptank River around 1908. The large, Victorian-style buildings in the background include the circa 1889 Calvin Satterfield home, the Clark General Store, and the summer home of A.A. Christian. (photo ~Hugh R. Butler collection)

Choptank River Boat Excursion. Captain Benjamin House takes passengers on an excursion on the Choptank River around 1880. (photo ~Hugh R. Butler collection)

Canoe Ride on the Choptank River: The old wooden bridge, built in 1834, and Satterfield's granaries and warehouses are visible in this 1880's view. The unidentified woman in the photograph sets out for a relaxing day on the river. (photo ~Hugh R. Butler collection)

126

Boating and Swimming on the Choptank River: Greensboro residents found many ways to enjoy the river. In the boat are Greensboro residents (L to R) Parran Russell, George Russell, and Henry Cohee. In the water are (L to R) unknown, Horsey Russell, Clarence Russell, unknown. The river played an important role in social life and enjoyment in the community. (photo~ Hugh R. Butler collection)

Choptank River View. This circa 1880 photograph is a view from the old wooden bridge, looking south toward the old "Brooklyn" section of town on the left and what is now the carnival grounds on the right. (photo ~ Hugh R. Butler collec-

View of The Last Wooden Bridge. This westward view of the early 1890's wooden bridge shows the original width of the Choptank River at Greensboro. (photo ~Hugh R. Butler collection)

Bridge Scaffolding. The early 1890's wooden bridge was replaced with this concrete span in 1907. The first step was to put the forms and scaffolding in place as shown above. (photo ~Hugh R. Butler collection)

Construction of Concrete Bridge. Construction was beginning on the concrete bridge over the Choptank River in 1907. The early 1890's span appears in the upper right corner. (photo ~Hugh R. Butler collection)

Early Construction of Bridge. This photograph shows details of the forms and scaffolding used during the construction of the 1907 bridge. Clark's Mercantile Store on the east side of the Choptank River is in the background. (photo~Hugh R. Butler collection)

Bridges over the Choptank River. Deteriorating conditions caused the need for improved roads and bridges. This 1907 photograph shows the construction of a new concrete bridge on the left to replace the old wooden bridge on the right. (photo ~Hugh R. Butler collection)

Concrete Bridge Location. The Charles Clark Mercantile Store enjoyed a prime location near the East end of the concrete bridge. To the right is the Addison A. Christian summer home, *Riverdeen.* (photo ~Hugh R. Butler collection)

Concrete Bridge Completion. Finished in 1907, the first concrete bridge provided improved safety and traffic capacity between the west side of the river and Greensboro's growing neighborhoods on the east. Another advantage was providing a quick route to Delaware. (photo ~Hugh R. Butler collection)

Greensboro Railroad Station. This circa 1909 photograph shows the unloading of building materials to be used in the construction of the hard surface road from Greensboro to Denton. (photo ~ Hugh R, Butler collection)

Roadway Construction. This 1909 photograph shows the construction of the first paved highway from Greensboro to Denton at Knife Box Road and Route 313. (photo ~ Hugh R. Butler collection)

Roadway Construction. This circa 1909 photograph shows construction of the paved road from Greensboro to Denton. (photo ~Hugh R. Butler collection)

Roadway Paving Equipment and Workers. Finishing the road in this circa 1909 image, Greensboro resident Walter Stevenson stands next to the steamroller on the right. (photo~Hugh Butler collection)

Steamroller and Worker: With the improvement of bridges and roads around 1920, local resident Harry Karcher poses beside the steamroller used during the surfacing of East Sunset Avenue near the concrete bridge. (photo ~ Hugh R. Butler collection)

STATE ROADS COMMISSION.

State Roads Commission. This circa 1932 photograph shows the Greensboro area State Roads Commission workers (left to right) Norman (Dick) Baynard, Bill Wirts, Bates Dill, Charlie Richards, Reynolds Brittingham, Bobby Walls, Charlie Dill, Harry Karcher, Joe Simpson, Edward T. Dean, and Edward G. Dean. The shop housed surplus equipment from World War I with one vehicle being used as a snowplow which had hand-operated windshield wipers and very little power. (photo~Miriam Baynard Binebrink collection)

Henry Cohee Family and Automobile. Another mode of transportation was the automobile. Photographer Henry Cohee and his family are seen out in their steamer automobile for a drive in the early 20th century. (photo ~ Hugh R. Butler collection)

Charlie Rich and Bicycle. One mode of transportation around Greensboro is by bicycle. This circa 1893 photograph (on right) shows Greensboro resident Charlie Rich and his bicycle with solid tires. (photo ~ Hugh R. Butler collection)

Greensboro Train Depot. A group of men are waiting patiently at the train station in the early 1910's. (photo ~ Hugh R. Butler collection)

Greensboro Train Station. This circa 1910 photograph shows a family in front of the Greensboro train station. Local transportation at this time was still primarily horse and carriage. However, trains had been providing longer distance travel for about forty years. (photo ~ Hugh R. Butler)

Passengers at the Greensboro Train Depot. The Greensboro Train Station became a vital transportation link for many Greensboro residents and visitors in the early 20th century. (photo ~ Hugh R. Butler collection)

Train Arrival at the Greensboro Depot. A southbound train can be seen in this circa 1912 photograph. Trains during this time carried passengers and freight. Goods would be unloaded onto horse-drawn carriages. (photo ~ Hugh R. Butler collection)

Horse and Mule-Drawn Carriages. The black pony (pictured on left) is owned by driver, Clinton Jarman, Jr. Mae Pippin is in the back seat. The mule-drawn buggy and passengers are in front of Hughes' Millinery that was part of the Horsey Building that was located on Main Street. (photo ~ Hugh R. Butler collection)

Greensboro Family and Horse & Buggy. This circa 1909 photograph shows an early Greensboro family about to embark on a horse & buggy ride in Greensboro. (photo ~ Hugh R. Butler collection)

Singer Sewing Machine Company Wagon. This late 1900's horse and carriage was owned by the Singer Sewing Machine business (Wheeler and Wilson, proprietors). It was stopped at the south end of the new concrete bridge beside Clark's General Store. (photo~Hugh R. Butler collection)

C.B. Jarman Delivery Wagon. Horse-drawn carriages were used in businesses as shown above. This horse and wagon delivered coal, lime, hardware, and furniture to customers. (photo ~ Hugh R. Butler collection)

Great Bend of the Choptank River. This circa 1912 photograph, taken from the balcony of the Riverside Hotel, shows the "Great Bend" with the concrete bridge in the distant background and the Riverside Theatre in the upper right. (photo ~ Hugh R. Butler collection)

Choptank River Flood at Greensboro.
Although its location in the middle of the Delmarva Peninsula generally protects Greensboro from the more harsh weather conditions along the Atlantic Coast and Chesapeake Bay, the town has not been totally immune from severe weather activity. The flood that hit the area on September 19, 1935, was an example when areas in the town near the river experienced unusually high waters. It led to one of the highest water levels in the town's history. (photo ~ Hugh R. Butler collection)

BUSINESS

&

INDUSTRY

Steam Tractor: Greensboro farmer George Russell (seen in picture) owned this steam tractor that was a top-of-the-line piece of farm equipment during its time. (photo ~ Hugh R. Butler collection)

Wheat Threshing. From its beginnings, the area around Greensboro has seen agriculture as a major industry. This circa 1880 photograph depicts farming methods of the era. (photo ~ Hugh R. Butler collection)

H. F. Butler and Children. In the past, as with most small towns, residents were allowed to raise animals within the town limits of Greensboro. H.F. Butler and two of his children are tending to the hogs. Note the beehive in the background. (photo ~ Fay B. Hubbard collection)

Blacksmith and Wheelwright Shop. In 1912, customers and their families are waiting for their carriage at L.P. Balderson's place of business located at the intersection of Mill Street and E. Sunset Avenue where the Riverside Gazebo is currently located. Three company employees are seen on the left. (photo ~ Hugh R. Butler collection)

Cohee Ice House. Henry Cohee owned this pond and adjacent ice house. He cut the ice out of the pond during the winter and stored it in the house to sell during the summer months. (photo ~ Hugh R. Butler collection)

Brockway / Riddleberger Mill. This circa 1950 photograph shows siblings JoAnn and Doug Riddleberger on the lawn. In the background is the Riddleberger Mill. (photo ~ JoAnn Riddleberger Dean collection)

Bilbrough's Feed Mill. This building (Jim and Martha Bilbrough, proprietors) was originally located at the intersection of Main Street and Sunset Avenue and known as Reed's Big Store. It was relocated circa 1901 to the north side of E. Sunset Avenue near the present location of Bodie's Market. It served as a livery station and feed mill. The building was demolished in the 1960's. (photo ~ Hugh R. Butler collection)

Wyatt's Feed Store. Oscar Wyatt's feed store appears on the left with Alvin Smith's Beer Parlor on the right at the Manz Beer sign. Wilbur Carroll's Garage is located farther down the road at the Texaco sign. Joe Simpson's grocery store is found in left center beyond Wyatt's Feed Store. The photo was taken from the porch of the *Enterprise* newspaper office. (photo ~ Hugh R. Butler collection)

Bilbrough Brickyard. This business was located on Bilbrough Road between Boyce Mill Road and Drapers' Mill Road. One of the largest buildings that the brickyard supplied bricks to is the St. Paul's United Methodist Church located on W. Sunset Avenue. (photo ~ Hugh R. Butler collection)

Butler Lumber Yard. This photograph shows another example of a business in Greensboro that provided building materials to the construction trade. The lumber yard (Charles Butler, proprietor) was located at 542 Boyce Mill Road. (photo ~ Hugh R. Butler collection)

Brockway Mill. Built around 1904, the Brockway Mill was located on the river near Riverview Lane. Captain Daniel S. Brockway, proprietor, was a prominent businessman with many enterprises. (photo ~ Hugh R. Butler collection)

Working Inside the Brockway Mill. Charlie Rich (left) is hard at work at the Brockway Mill around 1904. The mill provided employment for many of Greensboro's residents. (photo ~ Hugh R. Butler collection)

Charles Clark Mercantile Store. This store was situated in a prime location at the end of the Choptank River bridge. The original building was built by Captain John Allen and subsequently was owned by his sons-in-law, William C. Satterfield and George H. Moore. During that time period, the store was known as *Satterfield & Moore's Mercantile.* The store was destroyed by fire prior to 1904 and was rebuilt, owned, and operated by Charles Clark. (photo ~ Hugh R. Butler collection)

Interior of Satterfield & Moore's Mercantile Store. Retailers played a vital role in the day-to-day lives of residents. This circa 1900 photograph reveals the interior of the *Satterfield & Moore Mercantile* that provided a diversified line of goods for customers. (photo ~ Hugh R. Butler collection)

Hobbs' General Store. General merchandise stores remained popular through the middle of the 20th century. Burt Hobbs stands in front of his general store, which was located at West Sunset and Granby Streets. Customers had to shop early in the day due to the lack of lights inside the store. The building was destroyed by fire in 1952. (photo ~ Hugh R. Butler collection)

Rairigh and Brumbaugh Store. The Rairigh and Brumbaugh Store, later the A.W. Brumbaugh Department Store, was located at 114 N. Main Street. It was a shopping destination for the central Delmarva region from 1910 to the 1950's. It is the current location of Gray's Gas & Appliances. (photo ~ Hugh R. Butler collection)

Greensboro Millinery Shop. In this circa 1910 view of W. Sunset Avenue, customers enjoy a day of shopping at the millinery shop shown in the far left. (photo ~ Hugh R. Butler collection)

Main Street Businesses. This circa 1937 view of Main Street shows (L to R) Brumbaugh's Store, Fox's 5 & 10 Store, Bishop's Drug Store, Jesse Porter's Office, Hughes' Hat Shop, Doctor's Office, Jackson's Jewelry Store (later to become Cupid Ice Cream Parlor), Frampton's Meat Shop, Annie Edwards' Restaurant (later to become Butler's Barber Shop), and Atlantic & Pacific Grocery Store. (photo ~ Hugh R. Butler collection)

Downnes Cut Rate Drugs. This circa 1920 photograph shows the drug store that was located on N. Main Street which later became Potsy's Snack Bar — now a parking lot. (photo ~ Hugh R. Butler collection)

Interior of Dr. Goldsborough's Pharmacy. This circa 1900 photograph shows the interior of Goldsborough's Pharmacy. In later years, this became the left side of Potsy's Snack Bar on Main Street between Stoneseifer Drive and Sunset Avenue. (photo ~ Hugh R. Butler collection)

Free Press Staff. This circa 1890 photograph shows Residen Plummer (seated on left) and the staff of the *Free Press*, Greensboro's first newspaper. The publication was established by Addison A. Christian in 1880. (photo ~ Hugh R. Butler collection)

Greensboro Free Press. John Dukes Plummer (foreground) and Residen Plummer (background) published the Greensboro *Free Press* out of the second floor of the Horsey Building at NE corner of the intersection of Main Street and Sunset Avenue. The *Enterprise*, Greensboro's second newspaper, was printed at 100 E. Sunset Avenue between 1918 and 1942. (photo ~ Hugh R. Butler collection)

Wilson Thornton. An employee of the Greensboro *Enterprise* newspaper , Wilson Thorn-ton, is operating the linotype machine in this circa 1935 photograph. (photo ~ Miriam Baynard Binebrick)

Horsey Building. The Greensboro *Free Press* and *Enterprise* newspapers operated from the second floor of this building that was located on N. Main Street. In the foreground are the *Hughes' Millinery* and *Turpin Drug Store.* It is the current parking lot of a convenience store. (photo ~ Hugh R. Butler collection)

Helvetia Milk Condensing Plant. The company began its operations in Highland, Illinois in 1885 and established a manufacturing facility in Greensboro in 1920. It proved to be a major employer to the area until 1971 and a major revenue source for local dairy farmers for many decades. (photo ~ Hugh R. Butler collection)

Quality Ice Cream Company: This company was the forerunner of the Cupid Ice Cream Company and was located on the east side of what is now Industry Lane. To the right is the new Helvetia (later Pet Milk) condensed milk plant, one of the largest employers in Greensboro from 1919 to 1971. (photo ~ Carlton Porter collection)

Greensboro Bakery. Bakeries thrived in the Greensboro area around 1920. The second truck on the far right named Harrington, another local bakery. This house is located on N. Main Street across from the Greensboro Barber Shop and has been recently renovated by Mr. Brad Edwards. (photo ~ Hugh R. Butler collection)

Hennings Bakery. This bakery was a popular store in Greensboro. Mack Mitchell sits in the carriage, while Fred Hennings, proprietor, stands to the left in a white apron. The building was located on the southwest corner of Bernard Avenue and N. Main Street and later became the residence of the Calvin Butler family. (photo ~ Hugh R. Butler collection)

Riverside Hotel. In 1912, C.B. Jarman renovated to the old A. B. Roe Cannery to create the *Riverside Hotel.* This hotel was frequently filled to capacity in the early 20th century, when trains brought many traveling salesmen to Greensboro. The crossing walk was laid in order to allow Jarman family members to cross the street from their home to the hotel without walking in the mud. (photo ~ Hugh R. Butler collection)

Rear View of Riverside Hotel. A boat house and a garage are located on the property in back of the hotel and were used by guests. The Jarman family home is to the left in this circa 1912 photograph. The spire of the Methodist Church and water tower are seen to the right of the hotel. (photo ~ Hugh R. Butler collection)

Lobby of Riverside Hotel. The lobby is described as "the spacious lower hall of the *Riverside Hotel*." Guests who enter today will find that the main lobby has changed little from its original construction. (photo ~ Hugh R. Butler collection)

Greensboro Hotels. This circa 1906 photograph looking North from the intersection of Main Street and Sunset Avenue (the "four corners") shows two of the four hotels in the foreground that were established in Greensboro. Hotels enabled many businessmen in the early 20th century to conduct business in various towns. (photo ~ Hugh R. Butler collection)

Photo at right is a Westside view of the Nashold Service Station. Bud, Jack, and Beverly Nashold are shown in this circa 1930 photograph. It is the current location of Kinnamon's convenience store and Exxon station at the intersection of Routes 313 and 314. (photo~Gale P. Nashold collection)

Nashold Service Station. This circa 1930 photograph shows (left to right) Jack Nashold, Bud Nashold, unidentified woman, Barney Nashold, and Devereaux Nashold (in window). This service station was a typical drive-through style popular with gas stations in the early and mid 20th century. Pictured in the left background is the original home of William C. Satterfield, a local entrepreneur from the mid to late 1800's. It was subsequently the home of Fred Monroe of Greensboro Scrapple followed by the family of Earl Minner. The home has been torn down. (photo ~ Gale P. Nashold collection)

Currency. Pictured above are examples of paper currency that was printed in the 1860s by Farmers and Merchants Bank of Greensborough, the town's first financial institution. Bank President Spencer Hitch, whose signature is on the currency, is buried in the Methodist Cemetery on N. Main Street. Banks were allowed to print their own currency until such time as the United States developed a national paper currency. (documents ~ Bill Gray collection)

Caroline County Bank. This circa 1920 photograph shows the Caroline County Bank at Four Corners in Greensboro (intersection of Main Street and Sunset Avenue). The cornerstone reflects when the building was originally constructed. The bank has undergone many renovations throughout the past century and is currently the location of BB&T Bank. Part of the bank steps have been relocated to the Greensboro Museum at 114 W. Sunset Avenue. (photo ~ Hugh R. Butler collection)

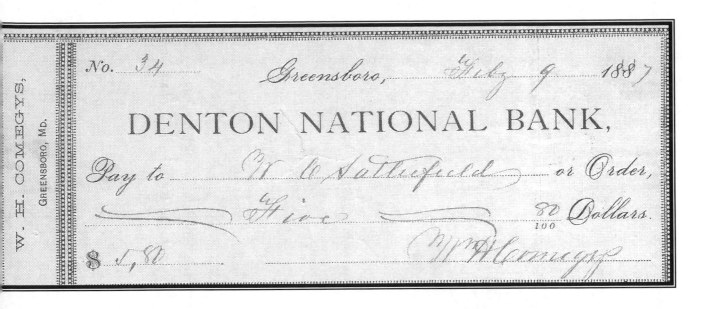

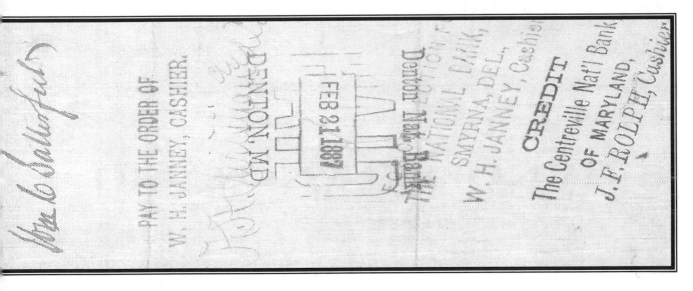

William H. Comegys Check. This 1887 check was written on the account of William H. Comegys and was payable to William C. Satterfield. It is one of the few documents in Greensboro's historical collection that bears the signatures of two of the men who figured prominently in furthering the early development of the town. (document ~ Hugh R. Butler collection)

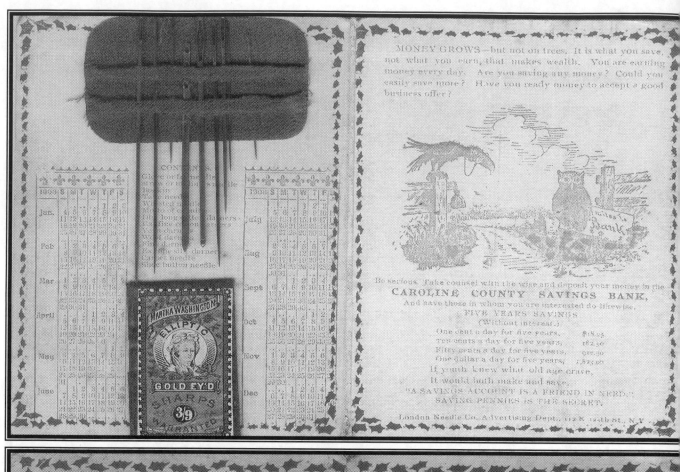

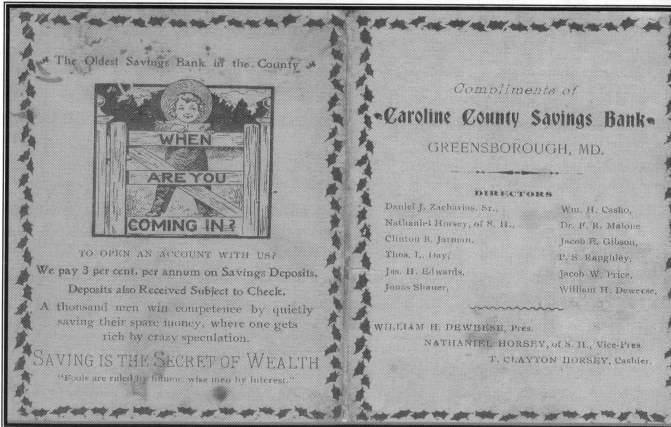

Bank Giveaway. This was a promotional giveaway at the end of their first year in business for the Caroline County Bank in Greensboro. (photo ~ Hugh R. Butler collection)

Van Sant's Drug Store. The drug store of Dr. Warren Van Sant is behind these two Greensboro residents, circa 1935. On the bicycle is Calvin Butler who was a barber in town for many years. The drug store was located on S. Main Street in the building formerly occupied by The Greensboro Trading Company. (photo ~ Fay Hubbard collection)

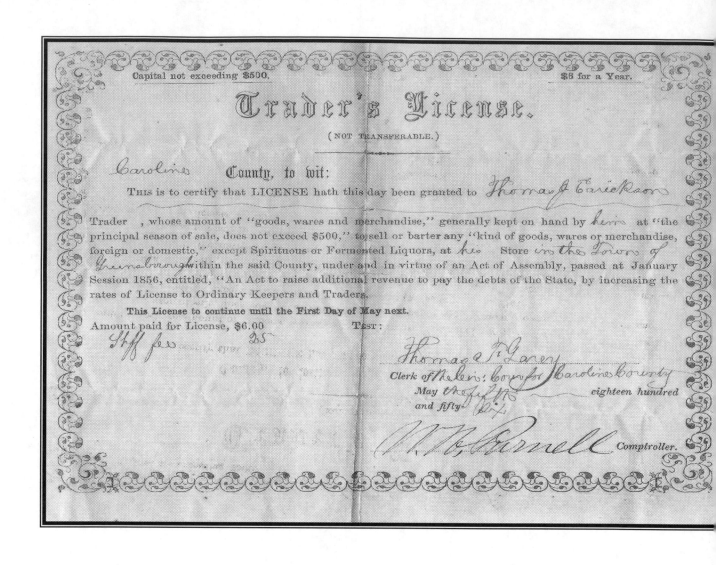

Trader's License. This is one of the earliest records of a trader's license dated 1856. It was issued to Thomas J. Earickson, allowing him to sell or barter any kind of goods in Greensboro except liquors. (document ~ Hugh R. Butler collection)

Sports Equipment Factory. Algren Manufacturing Co. broke ground in Greensboro to establish a sports equipment factory in 1910. It was a branch plant of A.J. Reach Co. of Philadelphia, Pennsylvania between 1911 and 1936. During World War I, it operated as a government-contracted supplier of tents for soldiers in the field. A.J. Reach's son, George A. Reach, acquired the business in 1937 and declared his business was not affiliated with any other corporation. The Geo. A. Reach Co. factory was in the sporting equipment business until 1958 when it was purchased by Hutch Sports USA that moved the operations to Ohio and Japan. (photo ~ Hugh R. Butler collection)

Making Baseball Gloves. These photographs show employees (Joe Riddleberger; left and Florence Thornton, below) of the Geo. A. Reach Co. glove factory making baseball gloves. The factory employed many Greensboro area residents until the business was sold to a company that moved operations out of Maryland. (photos~Jeanie Gardner Warren)

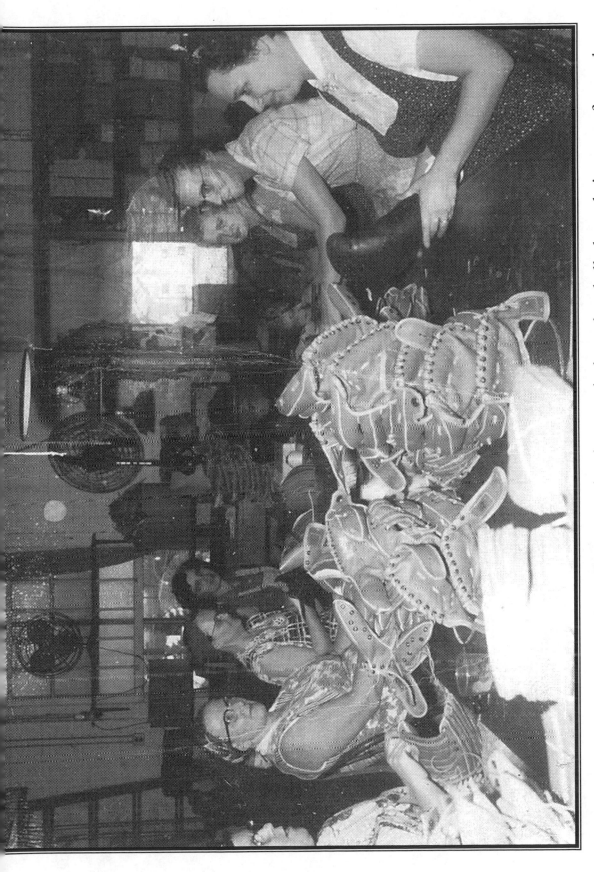

Employees of the George A. Reach "Glove Factory". The photograph shows baseball gloves being manufactured ca 1950. This building, located at Church Street and Cedar Lane, is now occupied by two manufacturers. Burkendine sheet metal fabricators and Joe Knaggs guitar manufacturer. (photo ~ Jeanie Gardner Warren)

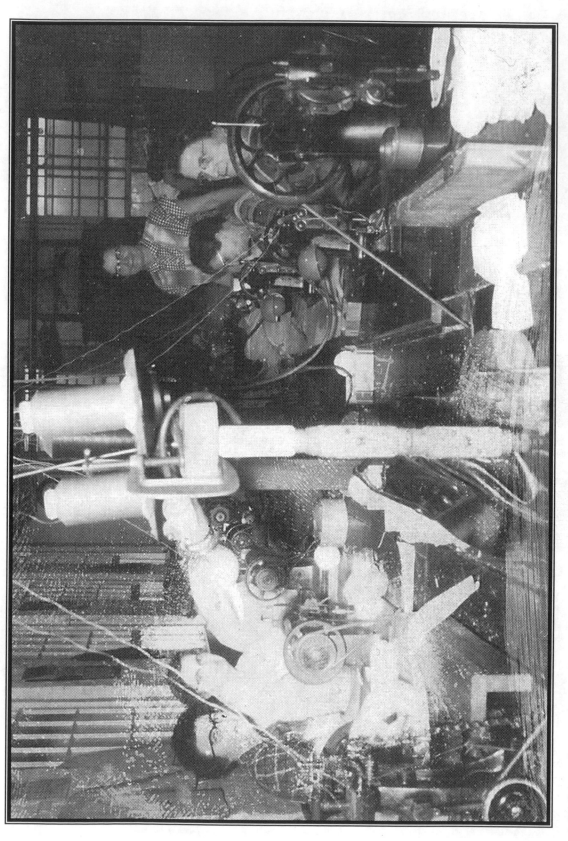

Sewing Machine Operators. Greensboro area residents were able to have steady employment with the George A. Reach sporting equipment factory at Church Street and Cedar Lane. George A. Reach's father, A. J. Reach, had established a similar business earlier in Philadelphia. The manufactured goods were shipped to colleges, professional sports teams, and stores throughout the United States. The Baseball Hall of Fame in Cooperstown, New York proudly displays some of the baseball gloves produced in Greensboro. (photo ~ Jeanie Gardner Warren)

197

Making Footballs. Reese Bickling, an employee of the Geo. A. Reach Co., is shown next to a box of footballs. The company also made football helmets, basketballs, soccer balls as well as baseball related equipment such as baseballs, gloves, wooden bats, and scorebooks. (photo ~ Jeanie Gardner Warren)

Grocery Store. This circa 1940 photograph shows the *Atlantic & Pacific (A & P) Grocery Store*. It was located on northeast corner of Main Street and Sunset Avenue. This location now contains the parking lot for a convenience store, (photo ~ Hugh R. Butler collection)

CUPID ICE CREAM

Price and Flavor List

****

½ Gallon · · · $1.00

Vanilla & Chocolate	Pineapple	Coffee
Vanilla & Strawberry	Strawberry	Lemon
Vanilla & Cherry	Cherry	Grape
Vanilla	Peach	Raspberry
Chocolate	Banana	Chocolate Chip
Fudge Ripple	Pecan	Orange Ice
Butterscotch	Walnut	

****

ORDERS WILL BE TAKEN FOR MOST OF THE ABOVE
MENTIONED FLAVORS

1 GALLON _____ $2.00
2½ GALLONS _____ $4.80
—Please Give 1st and 2nd Choice Flavors—

****

SOME FLAVORS IN 1 PINT CONTAINERS _____ 35c

****

Ice Cream Sandwiches _____ 10c each or $2.10 per carton of 24
Chocolate Coated Ice Cream Pops
                          10c each or $2.10 per carton of 24
Fudge Cream Pops _____ 5c each or $1.10 per carton of 24
Orange Cream Pops _____ 5c each or $1.10 per carton of 24
Fudgcicles _____ 5c each or $1.10 per carton of 24
Water Ice Pops (twins) _____ 5c each or $1.10 per carton of 24

****

HARLEQUIN BLOCKS (3 flavors - 6 slices) _____ 65c per qt.
       4 gal. and over — 55c per qt. on order

****

CUPID ICE CREAM CO.

Cupid Ice Cream: Shown above is a circa 1950's price and flavor list for Cupid Ice Cream which was manufactured in West Greensboro. A kewpie doll logo was displayed widely for Cupid Ice Cream. (document ~ Hugh R. Butler collection).

Cupid Ice Cream Parlor: Local young people were found socializing at one of the more popular businesses in town in this circa 1940s photograph. It was later known as Potsy's Snack Bar, named for the proprietor Mr. Potsy Flowers. (photo ~ Gale P. Nashold collection)

Goldsborough's Grocery. This photograph shows Beverly Goldsborough in front of his supermarket. The building is the current location of *Salon 39* on W. Sunset Avenue. (photo ~ Jeff Porter)

National Brands Store. Pictured above is the National Brands Store supermarket in 1938. Standing left to right is Joseph Riddleberger, Nelson Wyatt, and Mr. Coursey. It was located on the SE corner of Sunset and Main, the present location of the Greensboro Restaurant. (photo ~ Jo Ann Riddleberger Dean Family collection)

Swing Brothers Cannery Staff. The Swing Brothers' Cannery was one of the numerous canneries that were established in Greensboro during the early 20th century. It provided a solid means of employment to many area residents. It was later known as *Harrison's Cannery.* (photo ~ Museum)

W. G. Wooters Canning Label. The label for Mocking Bird Tomatoes was packed by the W. G. Wooters cannery, located in Burrsville and operated from 1911 to 1919. The child in the middle of the label is Bernice Wooters, the four-year old daughter of Mr. Wooters. Bernice became Mrs. G. B. Hastings and served as teacher and librarian at Greensboro High School for many years. She also established the libraries at North Caroline and Colonel Richardson High Schools. Mrs. Hastings passed away on Seprember 14th, 2010, she was 102 years old. (label ~ Bernice Wooters Hastings donated to the Greensboro Historical Society and may be seen in the museum.)

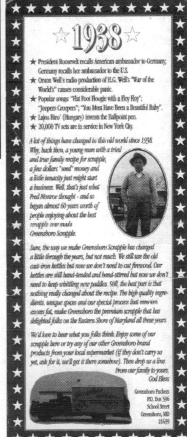

Fred Monroe. Established "Greensboro Packers" in 1938 on School Street in Greensboro. The Monroe family recipe for scrapple, the product for which he was best known, has been enjoyed for many years by the people of the Eastern Shore of Maryland and beyond. Mr. Monroe was a very active member of the Baptist church and a former Greensboro Town Commissioner (photo ~ Kay Monroe Dinkle collection)

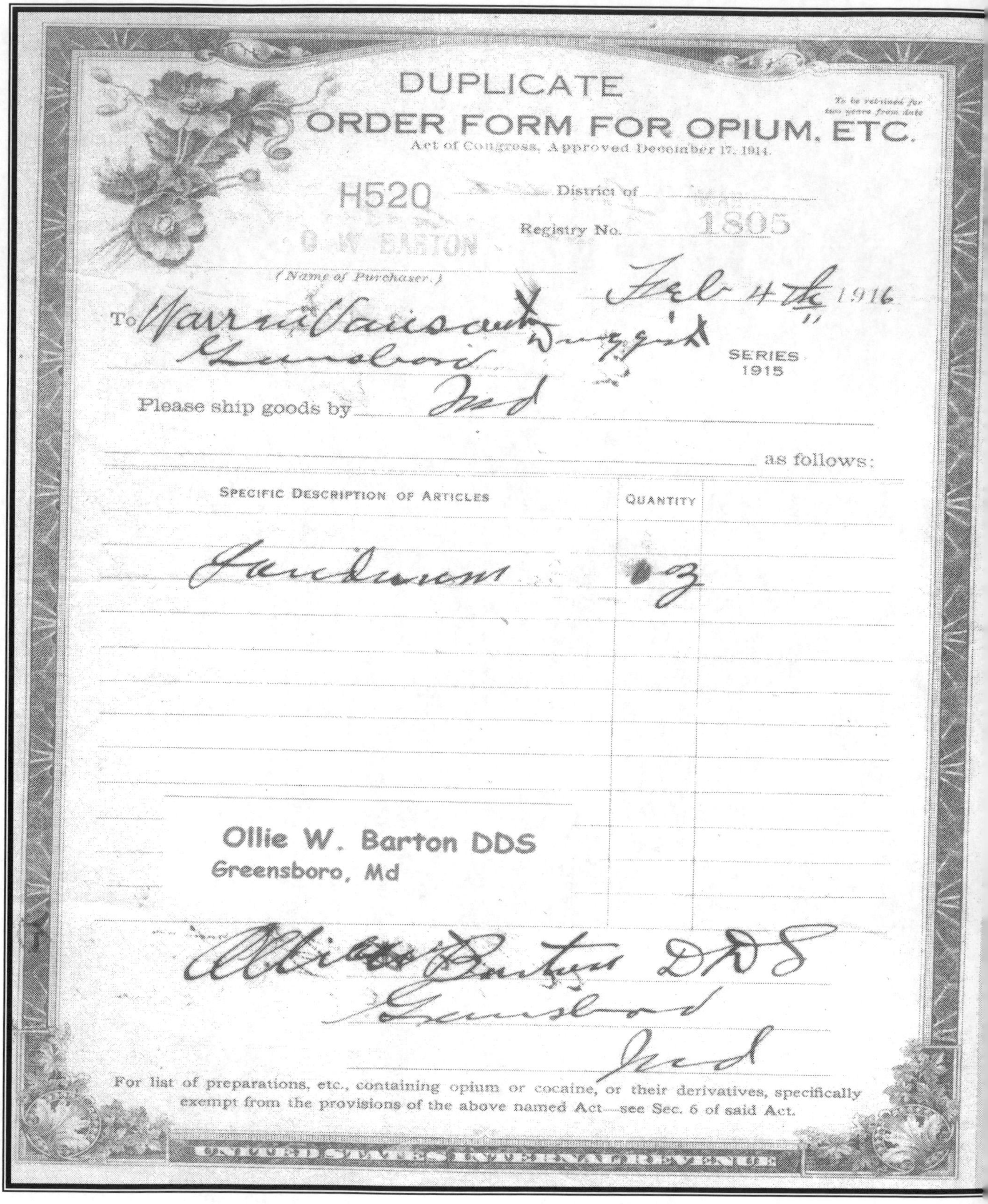

DUPLICATE

ORDER FORM FOR OPIUM, ETC.

Act of Congress, Approved December 17, 1914.

To be retired for
two years from date

H520   District of _____

O. W. BARTON   Registry No. **1805**

(Name of Purchaser.)

To *Warren Varis...* *Druggist*   *Feb 4th, 1916*

Greensboro   SERIES
1915

Md

Please ship goods by _____

_____ as follows:

SPECIFIC DESCRIPTION OF ARTICLES	QUANTITY
Laudanum	*3*

Ollie W. Barton DDS
Greensboro, Md

Ollie W. Barton DDS
Greensboro
Md

For list of preparations, etc., containing opium or cocaine, or their derivatives, specifically
exempt from the provisions of the above named Act—see Sec. 6 of said Act.

UNITED STATES INTERNAL REVENUE

Pharmacy Order Form. The circa 1916 document (pictured at right) is an example of an opium prescription that was ordered by Ollie W. Barton, DDS who was a dentist on W. Sunset Avenue in Greensboro in the early 20th century. (document ~ Hugh R. Butler collection)

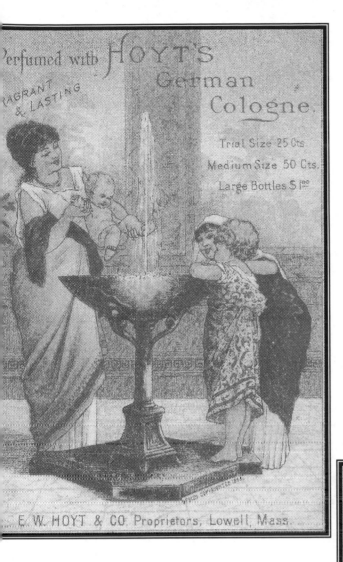

Perfume Trading Card. The card shown here (front and back) depicts the perfume trading card for Hoyt's German Cologne. It was sold by Dr. J. E. Lobstein's pharmacy on Main Street in Greensboro. It is the present location of Gray's Gas & Appliances. (photo ~ Hugh R. Butler collection)

THIS CARD IS PERFUMED WITH

Hoyt's German Cologne.

FRAGRANT AND LASTING.

This is the most delightful perfume known.

Its intrinsic merits have won for it a position above all other Colognes. Although it has hundreds of imitators, who try by Counterfeiting the style of bottle and label, to impose on the public,

No Perfume is like HOYT'S GERMAN COLOGNE.

Rich! Delicate!! Permanent!!!

Superior for the Handkerchief.   Unequalled for the Toilet,
Refreshing for Invalids.   Complexion and Bath.

To avoid imitations when buying, observe that the name is blown in the bottle; that our signature is printed in red ink across the label, and that our monogram cap over the cork is not broken. All others are worthless.

Trial Size, Price 25 Cents;   Medium Size, 50 Cents;
Large Bottles, $1.00.

Sold by Druggists and Fancy Goods Dealers everywhere.

E. W. HOYT & CO. - - - Proprietors,

LOWELL, MASS., U. S. A.

FOR SALE BY

Dr. J. E. LOBSTEIN,

Main Street, - Greensborough, Md.,

DEALER IN

Drugs, Patent Medicines, Chemicals, Fancy and Toilet Articles, Brushes, Perfumery, etc.

MILITARY

Private William James Patrick. At age 26, William James Patrick of Greensboro, Maryland enlisted in the military on October 11, 1862. He served during the Civil War in Company D, 1st Regiment - Eastern Shore, Maryland Infantry. He was transferred to Company E, 11th Regiment of Maryland and later honorably discharged and mustered out June 15, 1865 at Baltimore, Maryland. He married Mary Bedwell of Maryland. His son, McKendree Patrick married Mary Anne Knotts. His daughter, Daisy Elizabeth Patrick married Louis Henry Mietzsch and they had a daughter named Mary Lois Mietzsch. (photo ~ Hugh R. Butler collection)

Civil War Veteran and Family: Henry G. Rawlings, served in the Union Army during the Civil War. His wife and son Raymond Rawlings are beside him in front of their home in Greensboro. Raymond became Greensboro's undertaker for many years; descendants from this family still reside in the Greensboro area. (photo ~ Hugh R. Butler collection)

Letter to United States President Abraham Lincoln. R. Chambers, a Greensboro, MD citizen, wrote to U.S. President Abraham Lincoln in 1864 expressing concern about the behavior of Confederate sympathizers in Caroline County during the Civil War.

———————————————————————————————

Greensborough Caroline County M^d _T(?)._ Sepr 13th 1864.
To His Excellency Abraham Lincoln
President of the U States
       Most Exelent Sir
         Permit an humble unknown
in no Flattering terms but with entire candour
and profound respect to approach the earthly Fountain
of Wisdom and of Power in this Nation. I mean no
adulatory meaning when I say that such I look
upon the President of the U States now in office.
Sir
      We the Loyal Union people of the Eastern
Shore of Maryland are in contact constantly with
vile Secesh Traitors that frequently threaten us
with vengence when Stonewall Jackson comes into
the State. they declare that they have plenty of
arms in various places in this and adjacent
Counties. they have attempted and Swear they intend
to raise gurilla bands and companies; numerous
ones declare these things together with personal
threats against eminantly Loyal Citizens. we com –
plain, and in some instances the vile miscreants
are arrested. they are kept in durance a short
time they then agree to take the oath of Alligence.
and are liberated. they come home worse, far worse
than before their arrest; now, Sir. What is to be done
in these cases? Are we to bear the insults the T(h)reats
and the injury tamely submil to all and let these
vile Traitors go free? They have already but a few
miles from where I now write burned to (two) meeting
now. I apply to the Fountain of Wisdom and Power

(Continued next page)

houses or churches and others are threatened. it is true
we do not know who applied the Torch but
we know that it is justified by these Traitors
for advice what are we to do? must be(we) bear all
this and have no address? I tell you Sir we are
outraged and I believe the people will in this
most quiett and peacible County bear the insults
but little longer if those arrested are continued
to be again let loose upon us. We must and will
redress our own grievances. beside these we have
among us some men of some little wealth professing
to be union men, but are hale follows with the
leaders of Secesh and if we the people wont do
anything to organize and rally these men discourage
by their influence and words ridiculing them that
feel a Patriotic ardour, and in other instances say
if they had known that the District Emmansipation
bill had been part of the Palecy (Policy) of the Adminis-
tration they would not have suported it, and one
man a declared union man, on _Thursday last_
Since Maryland has been invaded and Pennsylvania
threatened declared he would be glad if the Southern
Army would get into the Free State. These Sir are
the vile Traitors we have to encounter at every
turn. again I propound the question, what are we
to do? I fear Sir that we have been so long and
so palpably triffled with that the sumary execution
of some of them will be the result; there is a mark
beyond which forbearance ceases to be a virtue and
at this point I hope the Divine Governor will
Himself bear rule.
With profound respect I am Sir your obedient
Servant   R Chambers

Conrad Rostien. This photograph shows Conrad Rostien shortly after joining the United States Navy in 1904. Conrad's naval career included service at China Station aboard a gunboat on the Yangtze River, Destroyer duty in the Black Sea and submarine duty during the early days of their development. He and his family lived on a farm on Greensboro Road about three miles south of town. (photo~Rostien Family collection)

Part of the Crew of the USS Stingray. Conrad Rostien is shown kneeling behind the life preserver on the day that both the *USS Stingray* and *USS Tarpon* were commissioned in April 1909 at Quincy, Massachusetts. These military warships became part of a submarine flotilla commanded by Lt. Chester W. Nimitz, who became Fleet Admiral C.W. Nimitz, Commander of the Pacific Fleet during World War II. (photo ~ Rostien Family collection)

1st Lt. Clyde "Brud" Embert, Jr., Ordinance Officer. This officer served with the 397th Bomb Squadron of the 6th Army during World War II. "Brud" saw duty in the Panama Canal zone and in the Galapagos Islands. (photo ~ Elsie Embert collection)

Alvin "Buddy" Simpson. This circa 1953 photograph is of Buddy Simpson who served in the United States Army. As many other home town natives would do, Buddy returned to the area after the completion of his service to our country. (photo ~ Buddy Simpson collection)

Two Sailors on Liberty. Greensboro native Devereaux Nashold (right) and an unidentified sailor are in the city of Shanghai, China in 1945. Devereaux spent his 18th birthday in this city. (photo ~ Gale P. Nashold collection)

Greensboro Boy To Participate In Atomic Bomb Experiments

Devereaux B. Nashold, S1/c, son of Mrs. G. Harrison Nashold, of Greensboro, was one of ten U. S. Navy boys stationed in Shanghai, China, to volunteer as a participant in the atomic bomb experiments in the Marshall Islands in July. The boys were sent from Shanghai to Pearl Harbor by plane, making stops of one day each on Okinawa, Guam, Kewnjolein and Johnston.

After reaching Pearl Harbor, young Nashold was assigned to duty on the U.S.S. Fall River which recently was made the flag ship of all the U. S. Naval forces participating in the atomic bomb experiments. Following is an article, in part, taken from "The Old Fall River Line" of April 24th, a bi-weekly ship paper.

In a ceremony scarcely noticeable amidst the usual shipboard routine the Fall River, three weeks ago, became the flag ship of all the naval forces participating in the recently-delayed atomic bomb experiments in the Marshall Islands this July. On March 27th the signal gang hoisted the two-star blue flag of Rear-Admiral F. G. Fahrion to the main yard arm. Many alterations had to be made before taking aboard Admiral Fahrion's large staff. According to the original schedule of the famed operation crossroads, the first bomb was to have been dropped about May 15th but President Truman announced that the tests would be postponed until, approximately, the beginning of July.

This week the Fall River is putting the finishing touches on the conversion which will make her the flag ship of the target fleet at Operation Crossroads. She was a ship which made a record to be envied. Today she is a big ship in the over all picture of the U. S. Fleet. Any ship that carries a flag has got to be good. The Fall River has lost a lot of men since shake-down, high pointers who came to her from the battle areas, from other ships whose fighting records are legendary. They worked hard for the records they made. They are watching us now, in the papers, as we take our first job which happens to be a very big job. When we leave this Navy we will be proud of what we did in it only if we do a job that is worth pride.

Seaman 1/c Nashold, who is eighteen years of age, volunteered for naval enlistment in March 1945. He has served eight months in China and will be returned to Shanghai on completion of his present assignment.

Minner Brothers, ca 1945: Pictured on the left is Nathan Minner, United States Navy.

John Minner, United States Army is seen relaxing below. (Photos: Marjorie C. Jarvis).

Bill Wirts. Once an employee of the State Roads Commission, Bill Wirts was drafted and served in the Army during World War II. Many of those who served in the military stayed in touch with former co-workers. (photo ~ Miriam Baynard Binebrick collection)

Private 1st Class, Howard F. Joiner. Howard Joiner was drafted June 15, 1944 which was one day before his twenty-seventh birthday. He was inducted on July 24, 1944 and sent to basic training in Little Rock, Arkansas. Following training he was sent overseas on the troopship Queen Mary that left the United States on January 24, 1945. During his attachment to General Patton's command with the 410th Cactus Division (Company D—Heavy Weapons), he walked from England to Brenner Pass in Italy. After being honorably discharged from the Army, many servicemen would gather for reunions. He hosted a reunion for forty former military personnel in 1976 at his home in Greensboro, Maryland. (photo ~ M. LaRue Joiner collection)

UNITED STATES OF AMERICA

CITIZENS DEFENSE CORPS
STATE OF MARYLAND

BE IT KNOWN THAT

NORMAN BAYNARD

HAS SATISFACTORILY COMPLETED APPROVED COURSES OF INSTRUC-
TION, DEMONSTRATED NECESSARY KNOWLEDGE AND ABILITY TO CARRY
OUT THE DUTIES THEREOF, AND COMPLIED WITH REQUIREMENTS
ESTABLISHED BY OR PURSUANT TO REGULATION NUMBER THREE OF
THE OFFICE OF CIVILIAN DEFENSE, AND IS HEREBY CERTIFIED AS

Bomb Reconnaissance Agent

AND IS ENTITLED TO WEAR THE INSIGNIA APPROPRIATE TO THE
OFFICE. IN WITNESS WHEREOF THE SIGNATURES OF THE OFFICERS
OF THE MARYLAND COUNCIL OF DEFENSE ARE HEREUNTO AFFIXED.

GIVEN AT BALTIMORE, STATE OF MARYLAND, THIS____TENTH____DAY
OF____DECEMBER____ONE THOUSAND NINE HUNDRED AND FORTY-_THREE_.

Henry S. Barrett
COLONEL, M. N. G.
STATE COMMANDER, U. S. CITIZENS DEFENSE CORPS

GOVERNOR OF MARYLAND
UNITED STATES DIRECTOR OF CIVILIAN DEFENSE FOR MARYLAND

W. Frank Roberts
CHAIRMAN, MARYLAND COUNCIL OF DEFENSE

W. W. Ewald
EXECUTIVE DIRECTOR, MARYLAND COUNCIL OF DEFENSE

Certificate of Bomb Reconnaissance Agent. This circa 1943 document denotes that Greensboro native Norman Baynard was certified as a bomb reconnaissance agent with the military. The course was given at Camp Meade and many felt that "they were actually at war with the effects employed." (document ~ Miriam Baynard Binebrink collection)

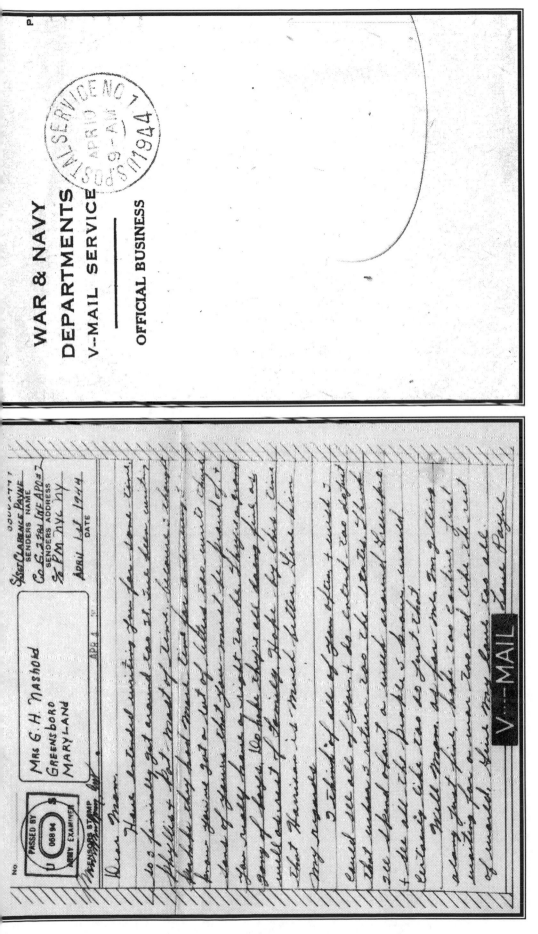

v-Mail Correspondence from Europe. In April 1944, Greensboro native S/Sgt. Clarence Payne sent a letter via v-mail correspondence to Mrs. G.H. Nashold. Victory Mail was a system for delivering mail written by those in the United States military who were overseas during World War II. After the initial letters were censored by the military, they were reduced in size and reproduced on microfilm. The film reels were then sent by priority air freight to a U.S. destination where they were enlarged and mailed off to the addressee. (document ~ Gale P. Nashold collection)

SOCIAL

AND

CIVIC ASSOCIATIONS

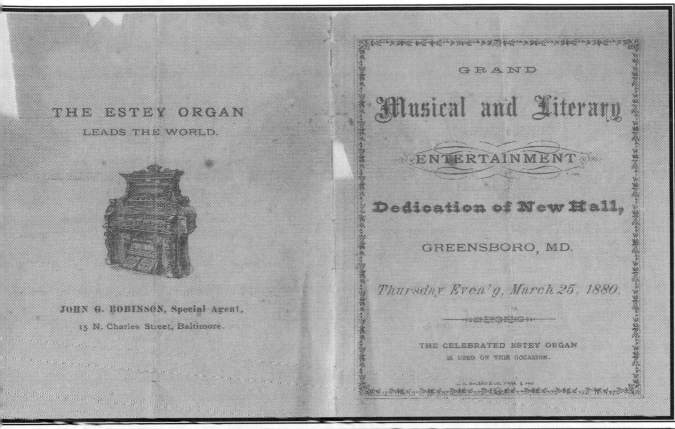

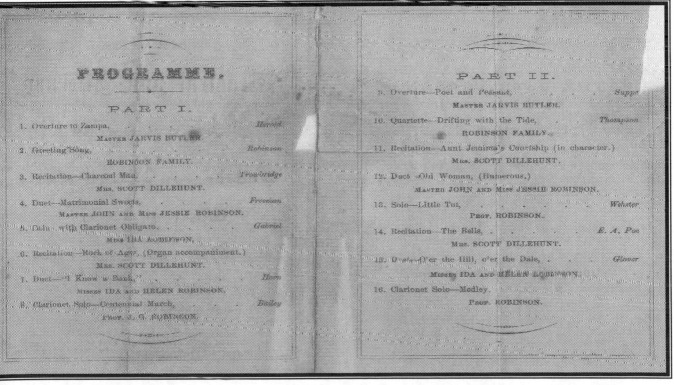

Mozart Hall Dedication Programme. The Estey Organ, played by John G. Robinson, was on display for the dedication of Mozart Hall in 1880. This theatre was the setting for many live stage performances. The building was purchased by A.W. Brumbaugh in 1910 for use as a Department Store. Present day Gray's Gas & Appliances at 114 N. Main Street in Greensboro. (photo ~ Hugh R. Butler collection)

Sleigh Race. This circa 1900 photograph shows the sleigh race in the snow down Main Street. The building on the right is a hotel on the East side of Main Street near the intersection of Main Street and Sunset Avenue. (photo ~ Hugh R. Butler collection)

Social Club. Men would gather together for supper club meetings held at the photography studio building on Maple Avenue in Greensboro. This circa 1890 photograph shows men enjoying oysters, whiskey, and cigars. This building has been moved to N. Main Street for use as a visitors center and mini-museum. (photo ~ Hugh R. Butler collection)

Greensboro Orchestra. Parlors were frequently the only available locations for small orchestras to practice as shown in this circa 1890 photograph. Pictured (left to right)—unknown, Ben House on cello, Brady Coursey Boggs on organ, J. Harvey Coursey on trombone, Robert Clarence Jackson on cornet, and Carelton "Ollie" Jackson on violin. (photo~Mable Riffle collection)

Greensboro Hobo Band.: Photo looking up N. Main Street from near the intersection of Main and Sunset Avenue. The Hobo Band phenomenon seems to have appeared during the first two decades of the 20th century. Dressed in traditional hobo garb with their unique mixture of patriotic songs, Broadway show tunes, seasonal music, marches, classics, and pop tunes, the band entertains young and old alike. It is dedicated community band musicians doing what they love. (photo ~ Francis "Sonny" Callahan collection)

Choptank River Fishing. One of the favorite pastimes enjoyed by men of Greensboro was fishing. This 1943 photograph shows a success catch by Mr. Beckham and Mr. Zacharias. (photo ~ Museum)

Deer Hunting Party. The success of the hunt is revealed in this circa 1890 photograph. Dogs were often used to help with the hunt in earlier times. Benjamin House (second from left) was one of the hunting party. (photo ~ Hugh R. Butler collection.)

Hunting Party. This circa 1890 photograph shows hunters with their dogs about to embark on a hunting expedition at the Cartwright Place on Union Road. The hunter on the left is Benjamin House. (photo ~ Hugh R. Butler collection)

After the Hunt. Enjoying the fruit of the hunt is an important aspect of the day's activities. This hunting party gathered in a barn for a wild game feast. (photo ~ Hugh R. Butler collection)

Greensboro Band. This circa 1908 photograph shows front row (left to right)—George Stevenson, Ralph Pritchett, Harry Bastian, Earl Nichols, Harry Karcher; second row—Harvey Coursey, Tom Thornton, Wallace Coursey, Howard Pritchett, Leonard Murphy, Russell Ober, Ralph Swann, Bates Wooters; back row—Mr. Ed Willis, John Stevenson, Edwin Willis, Charlie Koeneman, unknown, Claude Rawlings, Charlie Rich. (photo ~ Hugh R. Butler collection)

Greensboro Bandwagon. The band traveled in style from one performance to the next in this 1908 horse drawn mode of transportation. The band members would provide spectators a view of their fine costumes as well as their fine music. (photo ~ Hugh R. Butler collection)

Greensboro Coronet Band, ca 1908: Back Row (left to right)—Earl Nichols, George Stevenson, Tom Thornton, Leonard Murphy, Russell Ober, Claude Rawlings, J. E. Willis. Front Row—Bates Wooters, Harry Karcher, Wallace Coursey, Ralph Swann, Ralph Pritchett, John Stevenson, Howard Pritchett. (Photo—Hugh R. Butler collection)

Mary Pickford

IN

"Dorothy Vernon of Haddon Hall"

From the romantic novel by Charles Major Adapted by Waldemar Young

A MARSHALL NEILAN PRODUCTION

Photographed by Charles Rosher

RIVERSIDE THEATRE
GREENSBORO, MD.

MONDAY and TUESDAY, NOVEMBER 3
AT 8 P. M.

Benefit of Guild Holy Trinity Church,

THE STORY

DOROTHY VERNON, daughter of Sir George Vernon, is betrothed when a child to Sir John Manners, son of the Earl of Rutland. In later years a feud establishes enmity between the two families, and Sir George betroths Dorothy to her cousin, Sir Malcolm Vernon, whom she has never seen, and much against her will.

Shortly before the wedding ceremony is to take place Dorothy meets and falls in love with young Sir John. He has just returned from school in France and Dorothy, who has not seen him since their childhood, does not recognize him as the son of their enemy, the Earl of Rutland. When his real identity becomes known, and Dorothy finds she has been deceived, she tells Sir John she never wants to see him again.

Sir Malcolm and the Duke of Norfolk are plotting to place the beautiful Mary Stuart, Queen of Scots, on the throne of England. Sir John's father is tricked into this conspiracy and unwittingly involves his son by sending him to Lochleven Castle for Mary Stuart. In the meantime Dorothy's father has, at Sir Malcolm's suggestion, invited Queen Elizabeth to attend the wedding.

Dorothy, assisted by her maid, Jennie Faxton, resists the scheme to marry her to Sir Malcolm. Her father, realizing she is in love with Sir John, tells her the son of Rutland is a prisoner and will be tortured and hanged unless she consents to marry Sir Malcolm. To save Sir John she

Riverside Theatre (was located on the North side of East Sunset Avenue) . This circa 1920's promotional poster depicts a fundraiser for the Holy Trinity Church that was a production of ***DOROTHY VERNON OF HADDON HALL*** starring **Mary Pickford**. Ms. Pickford was a prominent silent screen film star in the early twentieth century. (Compliments of Doug and Barbara Mutolo)

Mozart Hall Tickets. Tickets to live stage performances were easy to come by. These examples are the few surviving tickets from a few of shows (*The Private Secretary* and *Dr. Devine*) that were performed at Mozart Hall in 1913. The venue was located on the second floor of 114 N. Main Street in Greensboro, the current location of Gray's Gas & Appliances. (photo ~William R. Gray collection)

Cast of Mozart Hall Performance. Performances that took place at Mozart Hall were often comprised of a cast of regional talent. The audiences were entertained with various plays and musical events. Front row (left to right)—Will West, Rose Harrington, Jim Tillson, Mrs. Brady Baggs, Mr. Wooters, Mary Butterworth; back row—Effa Plummer, Laura Letty, Jim Curry, Cordey Curry, unknown, Iva Jones, unknown, Will Mitchell, Watson Booker. (photo ~ Hugh R. Butler collection)

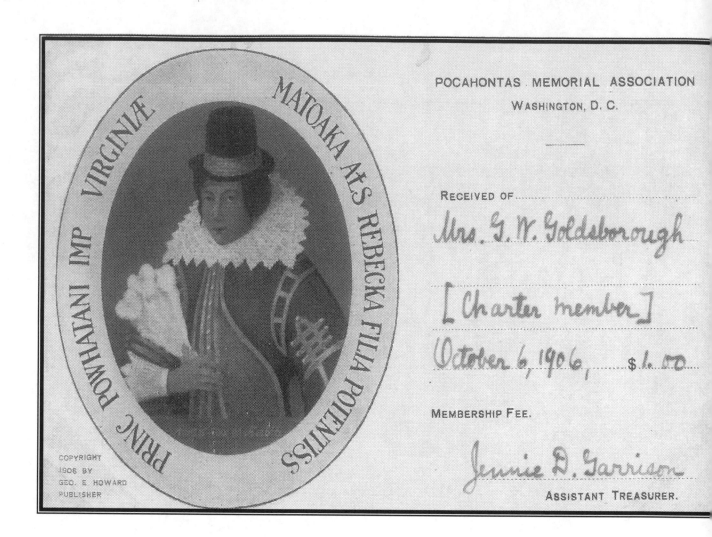

POCAHONTAS MEMORIAL ASSOCIATION
WASHINGTON, D. C.

RECEIVED OF

Mrs. G. W. Goldsborough

[Charter member]

October 6, 1906, $6.00

MEMBERSHIP FEE.

Jennie D. Garrison

ASSISTANT TREASURER.

PRINC. POWHATANI IMP. VIRGINIÆ MATOAKA AℓS REBECKA FILIA POTENTISS

COPYRIGHT
1906 BY
GEO. E. HOWARD
PUBLISHER

Pocahontas Memorial Association. Membership Card. Mrs. G.W. Goldsborough was a charter member of the Pocahontas Memorial Association. The Daughters of the Pocahontas was one of the social organizations that was active in the Greensboro area. It existed into the mid-20th century. (photo ~ Hugh R. Butler collection)

Daughters of Pocahontas: Dressed for the 1921 Fourth of July parade. The Daughters of Pocahontas was the Ladies' Auxiliary of the Improved Order of Red Men. The primary objectives of the organization were to "embody love and respect for the American flag, preserve the American way of life, keep alive American Indian traditions, and provide charity for the needy". (photo ~ Mary Lou Riddleberger collection)

Hunting Party. Several of Greensboro's business leaders took time to pose for a picture before setting out on a hunting expedition. Seated—landowner Mr. Knight; second row (left to right)—landowner Benjamin House, visitor Fred Quimby; third row—pharmacist Emory Turpin, landowner Calvin Smith, brick/stone mason James Nichols. (photo ~ Hugh R. Butler collection)

Kirby Metz, Sr. & Kirby Metz, Jr.
Father and son display the success
on their coon hunt. (photo ~ Kirby
Metz, Jr.)

Hunting License. This 1928-1929
hunting license was issued to Kirby
Metz. In the State of Maryland the
same hunting license was issued for
game birds and animals.

No. 7073   1928-1929

STATE OF ⚜ MARYLAND

RESIDENT STATE HUNTING LICENSE

This is to certify that in consideration of the payment of Five ($5.00) Dollars, the receipt whereof is hereby acknowl-
edged, license and authority is hereby given by the State of Maryland to:

DESCRIPTION OF LICENSEE:

Name....*D. Kirby Metz*....Age..*29*...Occupation..*merchant*

Street and Number.....*9*.....Postoffice..*Greensboro*

County....*Caroline*.....State..*Md.*

Color..*white*...Color of Hair...*Dk*...Color of Eyes..*blue*...Height..*5-6*

To hunt, kill or shoot such game birds and animals in said State, when and as allowed by law during the year
ending on the last day of May, 1929.

Given under my hand this..........*6*..........day of......*Sept*......192 *8*.

Game Fund...............$5.00   Countersigned by:
Clerk's Fee................25   T. CLAYTON HORSEY,
                                                                      Clerk of Court.

514 MUNSEY BUILDING, BALTIMORE, MD.   State Game Warden

1933 Champion Greensboro Town Baseball Team. Front row (left to right)—Pete Beaumont, Weaver Jones, Nuts Foxston, Harvey Dill; second row—Bill Snowberger, Jack Urry, Jimmie Holland; third row—Ed Walls, Lupe Andrews Charlie Bilbrough, Buck Bennington, Paul Dill. (photo ~ Hugh R. Butler collection)

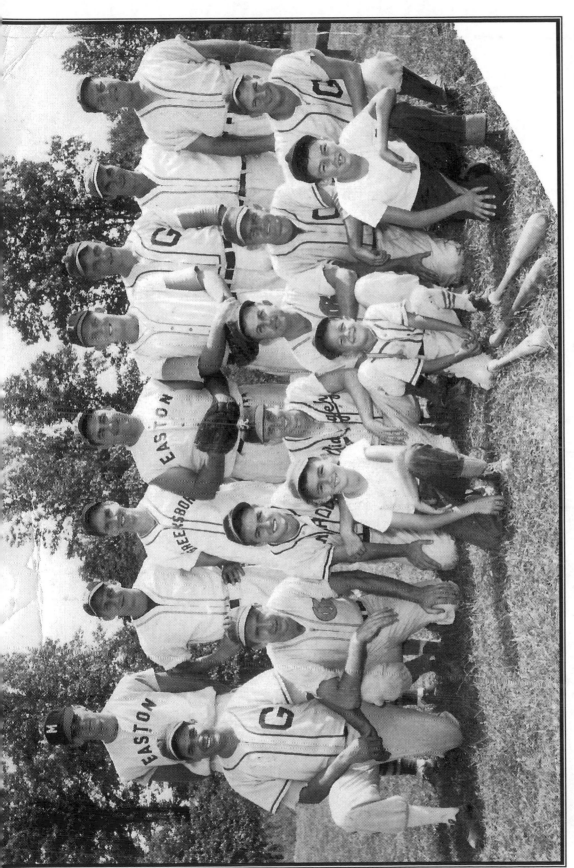

All-Star Baseball Team. Front row (left to right)—Henry Jarrell, Tony Giannoto, Jack Jarrell; second row—Tony Giannoto, Buddy Bennett, unknown, Chuck King, Eddie Dill, Dunken Webber, Buddy Simpson; third row—Tom Webber, unknown, Wayne Tribbett, Lenny Tribbett, Buster Caulk, Tomm Dullen. Jesse Chance, Med Shorts, Joe Simpson. (photo ~ Alvin "Buddy" Simpson collection)

Kirby Metz & Buddy Taylor: Kirby Metz (pictured at left) who owned the local hardware store, was the only Greensboro citizen to receive an aviator's license. Having received his training at Easton's Tred Avon Airport,, his first long distance trip was made to New York in 1929 in his Command-Are 5C3 airplane. (photo~ Kirby Metz, Jr.)

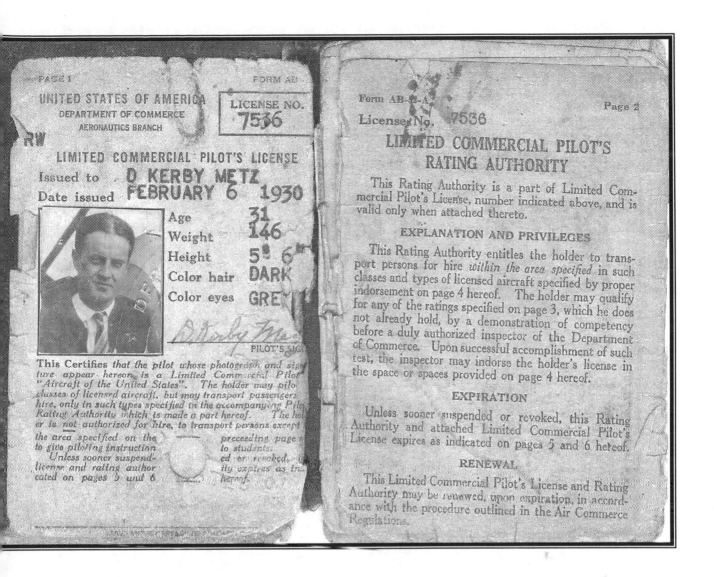

Pilot's License. This license was issued to D. Kirby Metz in 1930. Kirby moved to Greensboro from the Dover, Delaware area and purchased the Greensboro hardware business of Clinton B. Jarman. (photo ~ Kirby Metz, Jr. collection)

Parachuting in the 1930s: Spectators enjoying the daring of the parachutists in the field near the Greensboro Cemetery. (Photo ~ Kirby Metz, Jr. collection).

Lions Club Minstrels. This circa 1939 photograph shows Tom Edwards and Tom Thornton in blackface ready to drive down the Fourth of July parade route in Greensboro in their homemade vehicle representing the minstrel shows that were performed by the Lions Club. John Jarvis (far left) and Dick Baynard are seen standing behind the vehicle. (photo ~ Hugh R. Butler collection)

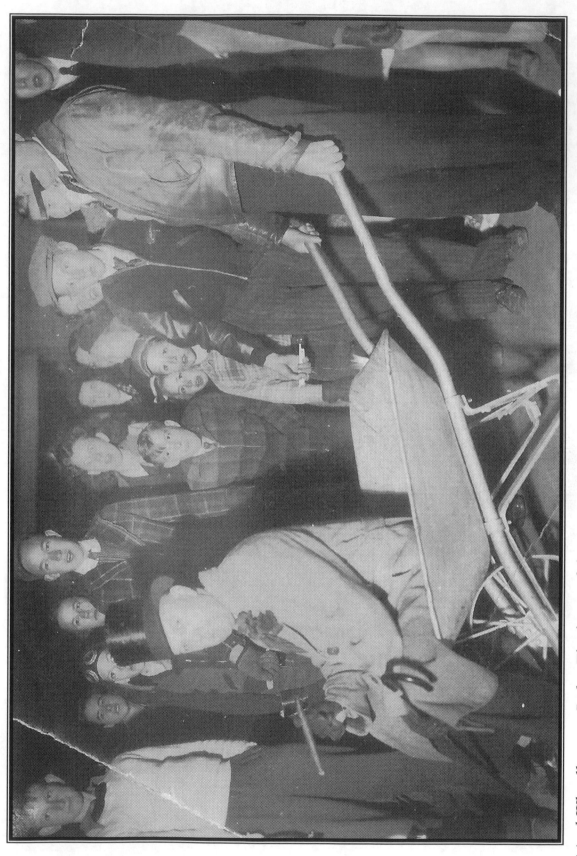

Political Wheelbarrow Ride. The loser of the mayoral election (Mr. Meekins) was required to push the winner of the election (Beverly Goldsborough) through town. It provided entertainment to the local townspeople to see the newly-elected mayor getting a ride in a makeshift mode of transportation. Greensboro elections are held every two years to ensure the chain of knowledge and experience is not lost when new council members are elected. (photo ~ Hugh R. Butler collection.)

The "New Theatre" on N. Main St.: When the top photo was taken in 1939, the New Theatre was showing a popular movie about Sam Houston, "Man of Conquest" (starring Richard Dix, Gail Patrick and Joan Fontaine) which had been nominated for three academy awards that year. Known as "The Little Theatre with the Big Hits", the building was located on the lot which now serves as parking for the old "Riverside Hotel". The bottom photo shows its proximity to the Riverside Hotel. photo ~ Hugh R. Butler collection.)

New Theatre Parade Float. The 1942 Fourth of July parade float sponsored by the New Theatre reflects the theme of World War II patriotism. Pictured (left to right)—Freedom of Speech, Ms. Usilton; Freedom of Worship, unknown; Statue of Liberty, Evelyn Usiliton; Freedom of Assembly, unknown; Freedom of the Press, Tillie Hobbs Schreiber. (photo ~ Hugh R. Butler collection)

Lions Club Parade Float. For the 1940 Fourth of July parade, the Lions Club created a float on the back of a flatbed truck. The District 22B Lions Club was charted in 1938. Pictured front row (left to right)—G. Alfred Gale, Irvin Johns, Linden Duffy, Russell Wright, Bert Kaler, and Raymond Rawlings; second row—Linwood Jarrell, B.L. Goldsborough, and Arthur Brumbaugh. (photo ~ Hugh R. Butler collection)

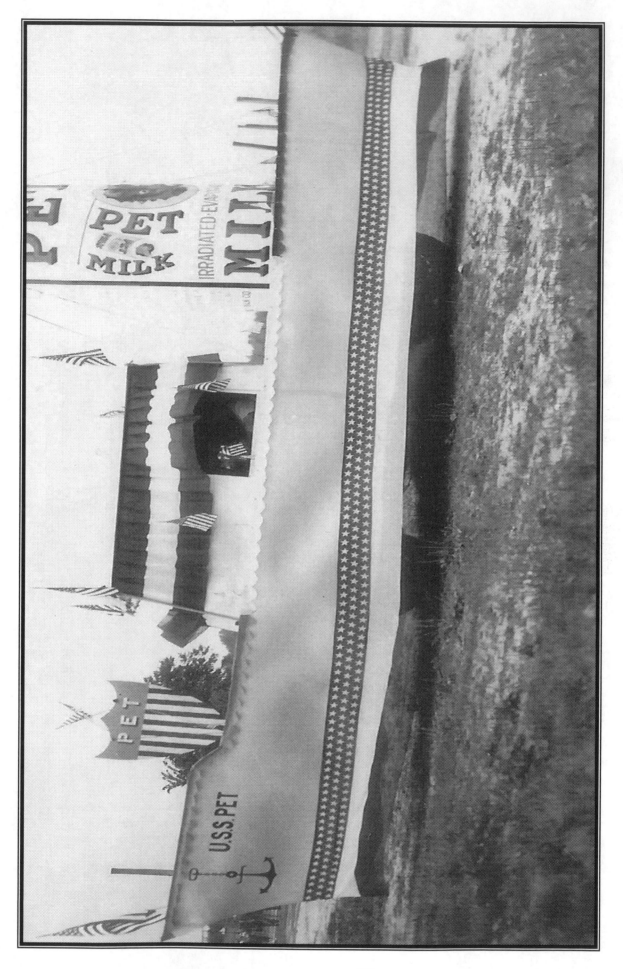

Pet Milk Company Parade Float. One of the major businesses in the Greensboro area sponsored this float in the 1942 Fourth of July parade. It was one of the more popular entries in the parade due to the continual support of patriotic themes that they decided to portray over the years. (photo ~ Hugh R. Butler collection)

Lions Club Parade Float. Elva & Larry Bilbrough sit on top of the lion on the Lions Club float that was often seen in local parades. The Lions Club is a community service organization that serves the needs of local communities.

Lions Club Minstrel Show. The 1945 cast of the Lions Club Minstrel Show. Performances were very well attended.. The entertainment included comic skits, variety acts, music, and dancing. (photo ~ Miriam Baynard Binebrink collection)

Uncle Sam and Miss Liberty. In 1916, spectators could catch a glimpse of Uncle Sam and Miss Liberty in Greensboro's Fourth of July parade. (photo~ Mary Lou Wyatt Riddleberger)

Fourth of July Celebration. The youth of Greensboro could be seen in old-fashioned costumes in 1948. Pictured front row (left to right)—Betty Jo, Diane Taylor; second row—Joyce Ann Nichols, Fay Butler, Janice Pippin, Barbara Butler, Donnie Jones, Charlotte Thornton, and Nancy Snowberger. (photo ~ Barbara Caine collection)

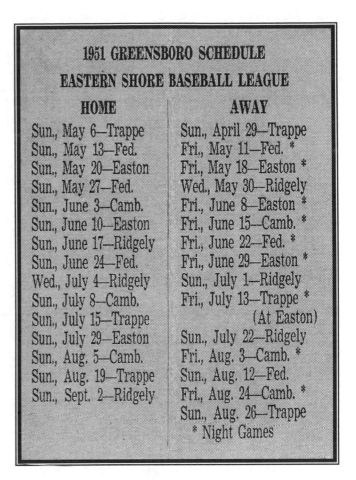

1951 GREENSBORO SCHEDULE
EASTERN SHORE BASEBALL LEAGUE

HOME	AWAY
Sun., May 6—Trappe	Sun., April 29—Trappe
Sun., May 13—Fed.	Fri., May 11—Fed. *
Sun., May 20—Easton	Fri., May 18—Easton *
Sun., May 27—Fed.	Wed., May 30—Ridgely
Sun., June 3—Camb.	Fri., June 8—Easton *
Sun., June 10—Easton	Fri., June 15—Camb. *
Sun., June 17—Ridgely	Fri., June 22—Fed. *
Sun., June 24—Fed.	Fri., June 29—Easton *
Wed., July 4—Ridgely	Sun., July 1—Ridgely
Sun., July 8—Camb.	Fri., July 13—Trappe *
Sun., July 15—Trappe	(At Easton)
Sun., July 29—Easton	Sun., July 22—Ridgely
Sun., Aug. 5—Camb.	Fri., Aug. 3—Camb. *
Sun., Aug. 19—Trappe	Sun., Aug. 12—Fed.
Sun., Sept. 2—Ridgely	Fri., Aug. 24—Camb. *
	Sun., Aug. 26—Trappe
	* Night Games

Town Baseball Schedule. This shows the 1951 Greensboro town baseball schedule that was co-sponsored by H.F. Butler & Sons Barber Shop. (document ~ Gale P. Nashold collection)

1940s Greensboro Town Soccer Team. Front row (left to right)—Wilson Thornton, Clarence Pearson, Francis Robin, Clarence Kibler, Fred Spence, Lawrence Sipple, Leon Spence; second row—Bill Henderson, N. Miner, unknown, Bob Riddleberger, Ben Howard, Bud Smith, Ovid Langrel, Ralph Bickling. (photo ~ Hugh R. Butler collection)

Greensboro Boy Scout Troop Camping, ca 1951. Seen on a Boy Scout camping trip, a future Mayor of Greensboro and President of the Greensboro Historical Society. (photo ~ Museum collection)

Greensboro Boy Scouts. Circa 1952, back row, (left to right) Jack Longfellow, Donald Jones, Bobby Dean, Bobby Kenny, Bill Miller, Bruce Riddleberger, Hugh Williamson; middle row (left to right) Kenny Moyer, Allan Boyd, Tommy Kemp, Richard Mace, Larry Pearson, Greg Wyatt, Dickie Cheeseman; front row (left to right) Marion Dean, Jimmy Minner. (Photo ~ Bobby Dean collection)

Membership

CURRENT

MAP

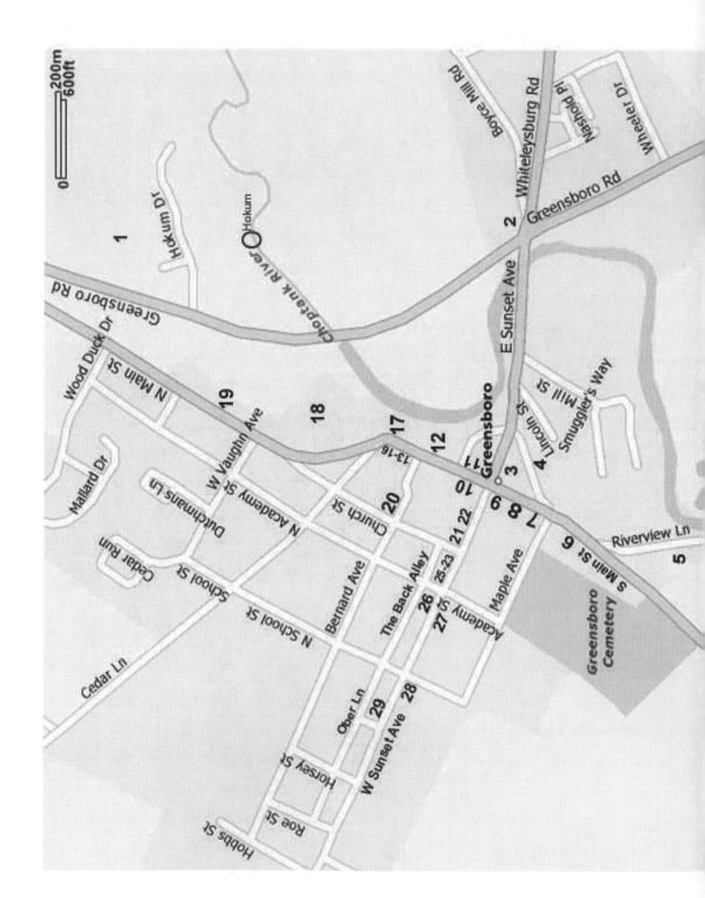

CURRENT MAP OF GREENSBORO

North Main Street from the "Four Corners", intersection of Main St. and Sunset Ave.. Hotel at left was on the present day site of the Bank. (formerly the "Caroline County Bank")

Proposed
BACK COVER